TOUCHED
by the
ANOINTING

TOUCHED
by the
ANOINTING

ROD PARSLEY

RESUL**T**S
PUBLISHING

Unless otherwise indicated, all Scripture quotations are taken from the *King James Version* of the Bible.

ISBN: 1-880244-64-0
Copyright © 2001 by Rod Parsley.

Published by:
Results Publishing
Box 32932
Columbus, Ohio 43232-0932 USA

CONTENTS

FOREWORD

We are living in the day of the supernatural. Everywhere you look God is moving with a mighty hand upon His people.

From the time of Elijah to the days Jesus walked the streets of Jerusalem, to the miracles performed through Peter and Paul, there has been a power available in the earth to set even the most helpless and hopeless captive free.

The anointing was in everything from Moses' shining face when he came down out of the mountain to his rod that parted the Red Sea. The anointing was present in Elijah's mantle as he smote the Jordan and the waters parted. We saw the tangibility of that anointing so strongly upon Elisha's bones that when a dead man was cast into his open tomb, the man's eyes popped open, and he lived again!

This same power is available to arrest even the most debilitating and life-threatening disease. Most of all, this power can transport a life from the clutches of hell to the glory of heaven.

Today, this power is available to every believer.

"And he [Jesus] said unto them, Go ye into all the world, and preach the gospel to every creature. He that believeth and is baptized shall be saved; but he that believeth not shall be damned.

"And these signs shall follow them that believe; In my name shall they cast out devils; they shall speak with new tongues;

"They shall take up serpents; and if they drink any deadly thing, it shall not hurt them; they shall lay hands on the sick, and they shall recover.

"So then after the Lord had spoken unto them, he was received up into heaven, and sat on the right hand of God.

"And they went forth, and preached everywhere, the Lord working with them, and confirming the word with signs following. Amen" (Mark 16:15-20).

The word "confirm" means to remove all doubt by performing indisputable acts of authority. It's time for the skeptics to be silenced. It's time for the doubters to cease doubting. It's time for the scorners to see a God who still performs miracles.

In this book I want to show you, through God's Word, that there is power available to you. God will give you motion against resistance—something called the anointing. It swells up out of your belly in times of adversity and propels you through every line of Satan's defense.

He gives you motion not to resist adversity, but to break through it.

You will go to a place you have never been before. You will begin to see things you have never seen before.

You will start to do things you have never done before, because He's about to empower you with a fresh anointing of the Holy Ghost. Isaiah 10:27 proclaims,

"And it shall come to pass in that day, that his burden shall be taken away from off thy shoulder, and his yoke from off thy neck, and the yoke shall be destroyed because of the anointing."

The yoke—oppression, addiction, pain, disease, hopelessness—is about to be destroyed because of the anointing.

At one time or another, the devil has tried to stop every person from receiving their miracle. Possibly he has tried to stop you even now. Perhaps he has waged an all-out spiritual attack on your healing, deliverance or the salvation of a friend or family member.

Jesus, the Anointed One, is present to meet you at the point of your greatest need.

The Gospel of Luke declares, "And he came to Nazareth, where he had been brought up: and, as his custom was, he went into the synagogue on the sabbath day, and stood up for to read.

"And there was delivered unto him the book of the prophet Esaias. And when he had opened the book, he found the place where it was written,

"The Spirit of the Lord is upon me, because he hath anointed me to preach the gospel to the poor; he hath sent me to heal the brokenhearted, to preach deliverance to the captives, and recovering of sight to the blind, to set at liberty them that are bruised, "To preach the acceptable year of the Lord" (Luke 4:16–19).

That anointing is tangible and it is transferrable. It will change you into another human being!

There is a remnant people who refuse to allow anyone or anything to stand in the way of their miracle. They refuse to be refused and deny to be denied.

Only Jesus can heal a sick body. Only Jesus can touch a tormented mind. Only Jesus can put a broken marriage back together. Only Jesus can give a ministry back. Only Jesus can give a person joy unspeakable and full of glory. Jesus came to a hurting and desperate world in search of you.

As you read the pages of this book, perhaps you will see a family member, a neighbor, a co–worker or even your own life reflected in the life of one of these ordinary people.

Desperation may have driven you to the edge of disaster. Disease may have caused you to careen downward toward death. Addiction may have arrested your hope and exalted your greatest fears. You may be the unlikely leader of a struggling congregation. You might be a desperate mother, a despondent father, a social outcast or feel as if you are just another face in the crowd. Whatever your station in life, you are about to come face–to–face with a loving God.

Deuteronomy 33:27 says, "The eternal God is thy refuge, and underneath are the everlasting arms: and he shall thrust out the enemy from before thee; and shall say, Destroy them."

Jesus has seen your tears. He has felt your touch. You are not lost in the crowd and He will not leave you as He found you. Reach out and touch Him. It's time for your need to be touched by His anointing.

1

THE UNLIKELY LEADER

And Moses said unto God, Who am I,
that I should go unto Pharaoh,
and that I should bring forth the children
of Israel out of Egypt? (Exodus 3:11)

For four hundred years the Israelites had served in the land of Egypt. However, there came a day when the reigning pharaoh did not remember the words of his fore-fathers concerning Joseph and his descendants.

So it was, during his reign, the Israelites' numbers began to increase to the point that, for fear of them, the pharaoh commanded that all Hebrew boys be killed by the midwives who assisted in their delivery.

However, because they feared God, they refused to follow through with his insidious plan. When his first plot failed, Pharaoh then commanded that the children be thrown into the Nile River.

Let me just interject this here: The devil has a plan to take you out but God has a plan to keep you in!

Through the cunningness of his sister, one small boy, a deliverer, was saved. His name was Moses.

It's a story as old as time. Moses was discovered by Pharaoh's daughter and grew up in the palace. He was educated in the finest of Egyptian institutions and protected by the pharaoh himself.

And, while Pharaoh was planning the extermination of the Israelites, God was planning their emancipation through the training of this unlikely leader.

One day, however, something went horribly wrong.

On the Run

Though Moses was educated in the courts of Pharaoh, he still possessed a keen consciousness of God. This deeply embedded standard drove him to sympathy for the suffering of his people.

Because of this, Moses murdered an Egyptian who was beating one of his Hebrew brethren. Moses' love for God's chosen people also compelled him to attempt the reconciliation of two Hebrew men. (Exodus 2:11–13.)

These two life–changing events drove Moses into exile in the land of Midian. There he dwelt as a stranger in a strange land. And there it would be that he would meet God forty years later. (Exodus 2:15.)

Meeting God

God found Moses tending his father–in–law's sheep

on the backside of the Midian desert. (Exodus 3:1.) The Lord will always find you no matter where you might try to go. He wrestled with Jacob at Bethel. He knocked Saul to the ground on the road to Damascus. (Acts 9:4.) He will find you too!

"And the angel of the Lord appeared unto him in a flame of fire out of the midst of a bush: and he looked, and, behold, the bush burned with fire, and the bush was not consumed. And Moses said, I will now turn aside, and see this great sight, why the bush is not burnt.

"And when the Lord saw that he turned aside to see, God called unto him out of the midst of the bush, and said, Moses, Moses. And he said, Here am I.

"And he said, Draw not nigh hither: put off thy shoes from off thy feet, for the place whereon thou standest is holy ground.

"Moreover he said, I am the God of thy father, the God of Abraham, the God of Isaac, and the God of Jacob. And Moses hid his face; for he was afraid to look upon God.

"And the Lord said, I have surely seen the affliction of my people which are in Egypt, and have heard their cry by reason of their taskmasters; for I know their sorrows" (Exodus 3:2–7).

A Long List of Excuses

In Moses' mind he was not ready for such a divine encounter. The Bible records that he was content to dwell in the land of Midian, and, therefore, had a list of objections to why God should instead choose someone else to deliver His people. Note the protestations of Moses to God.

1.   *Who am I?*

"And Moses said unto God, Who am I, that I should go unto Pharaoh, and that I should bring forth the children of Israel out of Egypt?" (Exodus 3:11).

Sometimes God, in His goodness, seeks out the least among the most seemingly unqualified, so that His grace may appear the more glorious.

Take for example, Israel's king, David. After Saul was rejected by God as king over Israel, He sent the prophet Samuel to anoint another.

Samuel was commissioned by God to anoint a son from Jesse's house. After examining each son and even thinking that one "looked like a leader," God admonished him not to look at their outward appearance because He looks upon the heart.

Notice that Jesse made each son pass before Samuel again. One son, however, was still out in the field tending his father's sheep.

Oh, think of it! The man whom God had chosen, though small and ruddy, was tending to the very treasure of his father's house!

God is searching for someone who will care for the sheep of His pasture. He is looking for a man or woman who, with His heart, will minister, with the anointing, to the needs and wounds of His flock! He looks upon the heart—the character and moral stature—of a person!

When David entered the room he was then anointed king, as Saul's successor, who had been rejected. (See 1 Samuel 16:1,6,7,10–13).

Moses, though a murderer and an exile, was just the man the Lord was looking for. He was someone whom He could mold, and because of Moses' humility, he was the very person God could use to lead His people out of bondage. It doesn't matter what your outward appearance may be or your abilities or lack thereof. God will anoint you for service based upon the condition of your heart.

2. Who shall I say sent me?

Possibly Moses posed this question to God because he knew that Pharaoh would ask the question, "Who is the Lord that I should let this people go?"

The Lord's response was, "I AM THAT I AM: and he said, Thus shalt thou say unto the children of Israel, I AM hath sent me unto you" (Exodus 3:14).

The same thing happened to Jesus when His predecessor, John, was shut up in prison for preaching the Gospel and baptizing people. While he was there, he sent word and asked Jesus if He was the Messiah, or should he and his followers wait for another.

I like to describe it this way: Jesus sent John a telegram reading: "John, the deaf hear, the lame walk and the dumb speak. Let my works prove who I am."

Through the anointing of the Holy Spirit, I think it is time we answered the question of a scornful world and an untoward generation that asks, "Who is the Lord, that we should serve Him?" Is Buddha God, is Mohammed God or is Jesus God?

We need to give them a word: the blind see; the deaf hear; the lame walk; the dumb speak; marriages are put back together; cancer is gone; arthritis disappears; homes are reconciled; addictions are broken. It's not in the name of Mohammed. It's not in the name of Buddha. But it's in the name above every name—the name of Jesus!

3. *They won't believe me.*

"And Moses answered and said, But, behold, they will not believe me, nor hearken unto my voice: for they will say, The Lord hath not appeared unto thee" (Exodus 4:1).

God already had a plan to show forth His power and anointing through mighty signs and wonders.

"And the Lord said unto him, What is that in thine hand? And he said, A rod.

"And he said, Cast it on the ground. And he cast it on the ground, and it became a serpent; and Moses fled from before it.

"And the Lord said unto Moses, Put forth thine hand, and take it by the tail. And he put forth his hand, and caught it, and it became a rod in his hand:

"That they may believe that the Lord God of their fathers, the God of Abraham, the God of Isaac, and the God of Jacob, hath appeared unto thee.

"And the Lord said furthermore unto him, Put now thine hand into thy bosom. And he put his hand into his bosom: and when he took it out, behold, his hand was leprous as snow.

"And he said, Put thine hand into thy bosom again. And he put his hand into his bosom again; and plucked it out of his bosom, and, behold, it was turned again as his other flesh.

"And it shall come to pass, if they will not believe thee, neither hearken to the voice of the first sign, that they will believe the voice of the latter sign.

"And it shall come to pass, if they will not believe also these two signs, neither hearken unto thy voice, that thou shalt take of the water of the river, and pour it upon the dry land: and the water which thou takest out of the river shall become blood upon the dry land" (vv. 2–9).

Isaiah 8:18 said, "Behold, I and the children whom the Lord hath given me are for signs and for wonders in Israel from the Lord of hosts, which dwelleth in mount Zion."

A sign is an instrument that points individuals to something beyond itself. A road sign is something used to convey direction.

People are supposed to be able to look at you, as a born–again believer of Jesus Christ, and find their way to Jesus. You're supposed to be a sign and a wonder.

A wonder can be defined as the display of the mighty acts of God that only He can accomplish.

This ministry is a sign and a wonder. When I first began preaching, I wrote down in my Bible, "Lord, do things so incredibly great that men would have to look beyond humanity and look to God and say 'no man could have done this.'" That's a wonder.

4.   I am not eloquent.

"And Moses said unto the Lord, O my Lord, I am not eloquent, neither heretofore, nor since thou hast spoken unto thy servant: but I am slow of speech, and of a slow tongue." (Exodus 4:10).

Long ago there was a preacher by the name of Uncle Bud who had stuttered his entire life. One night during a revival meeting he was preaching, a group of men arrived and sat down in the back of the tent. They had come to make fun of this stuttering man of God and disrupt the service.

After several minutes of yelling and ridiculing during his sermon, one man stood up, and from his pocket he removed a small, white oval object. It was an egg.

With all the force this man could muster, he threw the egg right at Uncle Bud. He didn't see it coming but right before it got to where he was standing, the anointing came upon him and he bucked, just missing the egg. He was praising God the entire time.

All of a sudden another egg came flying his way, and the same thing happened. However, this time the egg hit a leader of the church right behind him. This man, instead of praising God began to cuss. Uncle Bud said, "When the egg h–h–hit me the p–p–praise c–c–came out. When the e–e–egg h–h–hit you, what was in y–y–ou came out."

It doesn't matter if you came from the wrong side of the tracks and can do nothing but stutter. God knows what He has placed on the inside of you and it is called the anointing!

"And he said, O my Lord, send, I pray thee, by the hand of him whom thou wilt send." (4:13).

Why was Moses so adamant about staying where he was? Perhaps he sensed that he would be scorned by his own countrymen when Pharaoh increased their burdens. The very people he would seek to save would ask him to leave them alone.

Notwithstanding, God would not change His mind. After all of Moses' objections were raised and all of his inadequacies were addressed, he finally relented to the task.

All of His life, the Lord had been preparing Moses to lead the Israelites when the moment arrived. Although Moses could have ultimately rejected the call of God upon his life, and even tried to do so, he finally submitted to becoming His chosen vessel. He was anointed and set apart for that momentous time in history.

God, through His anointing, will not allow you to stay where you are. He can touch you and change you from a spectator on the sidelines of history into an instrument of revival in your family, neighborhood or city. He can transform you into an unlikely leader.

The Rod of God

"And thou shalt take this rod in thine hand, where-with thou shalt do signs.

"And Moses went and returned to Jethro his father in law, and said unto him, Let me go, I pray thee, and return unto my brethren which are in Egypt, and see whether they be yet alive. And Jethro said to Moses, Go in peace.

"And the Lord said unto Moses in Midian, Go, return into Egypt: for all the men are dead which sought thy life.

"And Moses took his wife and his sons, and set them upon an ass, and he returned to the land of Egypt: and Moses took the rod of God in his hand" (4:17–20).

When Moses stood before the presence of God in the burning bush, God said to Moses, "What is in your hand?" Moses said, "It's a rod. It's just a stick."

It was a shepherd's staff. It was something Moses used in his work.

God said, "Lay it down."

After that it wasn't just known as the rod of Moses, but it was known as the rod of God, and Moses used it to perform supernatural wonders.

When God lays His hand on something and claims it as His own, He may return it in another form to be used for His glory, but it's never the same as it was before God got ahold of it.

God has claimed you for His own. Once He gets ahold of you, you will never be the same.

I believe there is something in the life of every believer that God wants to anoint. There is a quality, a talent, a characteristic which God wants to claim as His own thus causing a radical transformation, effecting change to all who are touched.

Perhaps there is something God has already put His hand on in your life. Possibly He has already spoken to you about it, and it's something that He wants you to turn over to Him. God wants to place His hand on you in a new way, so that you will be changed for His glory and, as a result, change those with whom you come in contact.

The Lord wants to do something in your life that is going to break the yoke of bondage, not only for you, but also for somebody around you. It might be speaking to somebody's unsaved relative. It might be laying hands on somebody who needs to be set free. It may be receiving a financial blessing; therefore, causing others to take notice and realize that, "If God can bless them like that, maybe He can do something for me."

A Modern Day Moses

Let me share with you a testimony from a pastor who was ready to resign his church because of the onslaught of attack from the devil—before attending one of our Miracle Healing and Victory services.

Pastor David, his wife and daughter, along with a busload of parishioners from his church in Greenville, Ohio, drove two and–a–half hours to attend one of our special services. He wanted them to experience the glory of God and the power of God manifested in healing and deliverance.

At the time, he was experiencing the most difficult time of his ministry. He was ready to quit, and he had the resignation papers filled out laying on his desk at home.

His wife felt his tremendous burden and was crying out to God for answers.

They didn't know that God had this special service planned for them. They thought they were just bringing their church group to receive a touch, but God also wanted to touch them.

During that particular service, I called out, "People bound by depression are being set free." Pastor David felt what was being said was exactly what he was feeling. I said, "You want to quit. Everyone would be surprised to hear it but you've been wanting to give up and quit." Instantly, this pastor felt a heaviness leave him and he knew the oppression was gone.

As if that wasn't enough, their daughter, Sarah, received a healing touch from God! Sarah was diagnosed with a hearing problem. The doctors said she would never be able to hear normally. After the miracle touch of healing, Sarah was able to hear even the slightest whisper. She was retested and the doctors said she is completely normal!

On the Precipice of the Promised Land

Picture Moses nearing the end of His life, leaning upon the staff which God had so mightily anointed and used in his hand to perform signs and wonders before Pharaoh and his magicians. Upon the children of Israel's exodus, that rod was stretched out over the barrier of the Red Sea where the waters were divided and a way was made for them to pass over. That same staff struck a rock and eventually kept Moses from entering the promised land. (Numbers 20:8–12.)

I envision Moses, now older and grayer, on the mountain of Nebo resting one last time upon that staff, as he looks toward the promised land. Forty years and many miracles later, the Lord has come down to usher Moses into His pavilions of glory.

"And Moses went up from the plains of Moab unto the mountain of Nebo, to the top of Pisgah, that is over against Jericho. And the Lord shewed him all the land of Gilead, unto Dan, and all Naphtali, and the land of Ephraim, and Manasseh, and all the land of Judah, unto the utmost sea, And the south, and the plain of the valley of Jericho, the city of palm trees, unto Zoar.

"And the Lord said unto him, This is the land which I sware unto Abraham, unto Isaac, and unto Jacob, saying, I will give it unto thy seed: I have caused thee to see it with thine eyes, but thou shalt not go over thither.

"So Moses the servant of the Lord died there in the land of Moab, according to the word of the Lord. And he buried him in a valley in the land of Moab, over against Beth–peor: but no man knoweth of his sepulchre unto this day. And Moses was an hundred and twenty years old when he died: his eye was not dim, nor his natural force abated" (Deuteronomy 34:1–7).

Jehovah, who displayed Himself to Moses in Mount Sinai, was about to meet with him face–to–face. God presided over the funeral of His servant Moses. The Lord of Hosts gave the eulogy. He buried His chosen vessel.

The Hall of Faith

Through the anointing, this murderer was transformed into a leader—an unlikely leader—used to usher God's people out of bondage.

Moses' reputation with Israel and relationship with God reserved him a place in the Bible's hall of faith.

"By faith Moses, when he was born, was hid three months of his parents, because they saw he was a proper child; and they were not afraid of the king's commandment.

"By faith Moses, when he was come to years, refused to be called the son of Pharaoh's daughter; Choosing rather to suffer affliction with the people of God, than to enjoy the pleasures of sin for a season; esteeming the reproach of Christ greater riches than the treasures in Egypt: for he had respect unto the recompence of the reward.

"By faith he forsook Egypt, not fearing the wrath of the king: for he endured, as seeing him who is invisible. Through faith he kept the passover, and the sprinkling of blood, lest he that destroyed the firstborn should touch them.

"By faith they passed through the Red sea as by dry land: which the Egyptians assaying to do were drowned" (Hebrews 11:23–29).

Maybe you feel even more inadequate than Moses or Pastor David. After all, in your mind, you are definitely not leadership material.

Let me encourage you that God wants to touch you with His anointing.

Through His anointing, you will gain acceptance, ability and authority you never dreamed possible.

In the same way God's anointing turned a stuttering servant into a powerful leader, His anointing will transform your life.

There is one important point about a leader to keep in mind. Jesus said, "And whosoever will be chief among you, let him be your servant: Even as the Son of man came not to be ministered unto, but to minister, and to give his life a ransom for many" (Matthew 20:27,28).

You may not be called to preach to the masses. You may not be selected to be a missionary in a foreign country. However, your greatest task may be, through the touch of God's anointing, to lead your family to the feet of Jesus. Perhaps you are chosen to minister to an elderly neighbor or a sick family member. With a servant's heart, God will make you the leader you may have never imagined you could or would be. God uses ready and available vessels to become the catalyst to affect a miracle, healing, salvation or deliverance in someone else's life.

2

THE STEADFAST MOTHER

Is it well with thee? is it well with thy
husband? is it well with the child?
And she answered, It is well.
(2 Kings 4:26).

Elisha is one of the most profound prophets of the
Old Testament. He was mentored in Elijah's school of the
prophets. He was a man who not only wanted what Elijah
had, but he also wanted a double portion.

Elijah was by no means a minor prophet. He raised
the dead. He slew the prophets of Baal. He prayed for a
drought to fall upon the land during the reign of Ahab and
it did. He even outran Ahab's chariots when dark–throated
storm clouds broke over the horizon.

This prophet smote the Jordan River with his mantle
and crossed over on dry ground. During the end of his
earthly life, he was taken up in a whirlwind in the chariot
of God.

With Elijah's heavenly departure, Elisha was now
positioned to perform twice as many miracles during his
lifetime as his predecessor. Even in his death the anointing was so prevalent upon Elisha's bones that when a dead

man was cast into his open tomb, the man's eyes popped open and he lived again! (2 Kings 13:21.)

The anointing will cause that which was once dead to live again! It is the life force of almighty God!

The anointing will mend broken bones, broken hearts and broken dreams!

The anointing will deliver the downcast and the desperate!

This chapter, however, is not about Elijah or Elisha. Instead it is about a mother, who through her steadfast faith, was about to experience the anointing of God in her own life.

A Chamber is Prepared

Second Kings 4 tells the story of Elisha the Prophet and a woman from Shunem. She and her husband had built Elisha a little room to abide in whenever he passed through their town.

"And it fell on a day, that Elisha passed to Shunem, where was a great woman; and she constrained him to eat bread. And so it was, that as oft as he passed by, he turned in thither to eat bread.

"And she said unto her husband, Behold now, I perceive that this is an holy man of God, which passeth by us continually.

"Let us make a little chamber, I pray thee, on the wall; and let us set for him there a bed, and a table, and a stool, and a candlestick: and it shall be, when he cometh to us, that he shall turn in thither.

"And it fell on a day, that he came thither, and he turned into the chamber, and lay there" (2 Kings 4:8–11).

The Shunammite woman and her husband prepared a place for the man of God. I like to think that Elisha was possibly passing through on his way to a revival meeting.

In the chamber, this woman furnished four items: a bed, a table, a chair and a candlestick. She made provision for the man of God, which ultimately sustained her.

The first thing that she gave him was a bed. Recently, the Holy Spirit impressed upon me that we must come to the place where the struggle ceases. Hebrews 4:9 says, "There remaineth therefore a rest to the people of God."

This woman in essence said, "I am going to give this prophet a place to pillow his head and rest."

Sometimes God wants to take you to another level of His anointing but there is a struggle taking place inside of you. However, God wants you to rest in Him and allow His Holy Spirit to do His perfect work in you.

Hebrews 13:20,21 state, "Now the God of peace, that brought again from the dead our Lord Jesus, that great shepherd of the sheep, through the blood of the everlasting covenant,

"Make you perfect in every good work to do his will, working in you that which is wellpleasing in his sight, through Jesus Christ; to whom be glory for ever and ever. Amen."

Second, this woman set a table for Elisha. The table represents the partaking of daily bread. It represents food or nourishment. In the New Testament, it makes reference to the breaking of bread from house to house.

"And they continued stedfastly in the apostles' doctrine and fellowship, and in breaking of bread, and in prayers" (Acts 2:42).

The Shunammite woman's house was tied to God's house.

She made her house Elisha's house so that when she needed a miracle, Elisha didn't have to ask permission.

He just walked into his place. We must make a habitation for God's Spirit in our heart, through the confession of our mouth, so that when we need a miracle, he can touch us with His anointing!

If you are part of a local church, you should be able to find nourishment there. What type of nourishment should be there? Jesus declared, "And these signs shall follow them that believe; In my name shall they cast out devils; they shall speak with new tongues; They shall take up serpents; and if they drink any deadly thing, it shall not hurt them; they shall lay hands on the sick, and they shall recover" (Mark 16:17,18).

The last two things the woman provided Elisha were a candlestick and a chair. The candlestick epitomized the illumination of the revelation of the Word of God. The Psalmist said, "Thy word is a lamp unto my feet, and a light unto my path" (119:105).

The chair represented the seat of authority. The Shunammite woman gave the man of God a place of authority in her life. She availed herself of his covering and protection.

The Shunammite woman continued steadfastly to serve Elisha, and her house became God's house. While she finished preparing a place for Elisha, God was making preparations for her miracle.

What Shall I Do For Thee?

If you take care of the man of God, God will take care of you. This woman wanted a son. Elisha prayed and God gave her a son.

"And he said to Gehazi his servant, Call this Shunammite. And when he had called her, she stood before him.

"And he said unto him, Say now unto her, Behold, thou hast been careful for us with all this care; what is to be done for thee? wouldest thou be spoken for to the king, or to the captain of the host? And she answered, I dwell among mine own people.

"And he said, What then is to be done for her? And Gehazi answered, Verily she hath no child, and her husband is old. And he said, Call her. And when he had called her, she stood in the door.

"And he said, About this season, according to the time of life, thou shalt embrace a son. And she said, Nay, my Lord, thou man of God, do not lie unto thine hand-maid.

"And the woman conceived, and bare a son at that season that Elisha had said unto her, according to the time of life" (2 Kings 4:12–17).

What most of us wouldn't give for God just to walk up and ask, "What do you want?"

Let me paraphrase this passage of Scripture for you. Elisha says, "About this season you will conceive a child. It is your time!" Did you notice that it was not the right season until she set everything in order? But when she set everything in order, it then became her season.

Elisha said, "According to the time of life, thou shalt embrace a son." She said, "Don't you lie to me!" (2 Kings 4:16.)

Sometimes God's promises seem too good to be true. You may say, "Oh, God, don't say that to me. I'll get my hopes up." However, the Bible says, "When the Lord turned again the captivity of Zion, we were like them that dream.

"Then was our mouth filled with laughter, and our tongue with singing: then said they among the heathen, The Lord hath done great things for them" (Psalm 126:1,2).

The Miracle Dies

This woman had conceived her miracle child. However, the life that had begun so supernaturally was about to end in sorrow. This mother's hopes had been devastated by an unexpected turn of events.

Second Kings 4:18–21 records, "And when the child was grown, it fell on a day, that he went out to his father to the reapers. And he said unto his father, My head, my head. And he said to a lad, Carry him to his mother.

"And when he had taken him, and brought him to his mother, he sat on her knees till noon, and then died.

"And she went up, and laid him on the bed of the man of God, and shut the door upon him, and went out."

Let me just interject this here: When my mentor and pastor, Dr. Lester Sumrall, was living, he would stay in our home while he was ministering at our church. We would try to get him the finest suite in the most beautiful hotel in town. Nonetheless, he wouldn't stay there.

One time in particular I asked him, "Why do you not want to go to that hotel when they have room service and everything?"

He said, "One reason. I want to sleep in your bed." He didn't want to sleep in my bed to get the anointing I had. He wanted to sleep in my bed to leave the anointing that resided in him—an impartation of the anointing!

After that I would tell my wife, Joni, "Just leave those sheets alone. We're going to sleep in the anointing tonight!"

Now the Shunammite's son lay lifeless in the room that had been prepared for the man of God. The child of promise was now dead.

Second Kings goes on to document, "And she called unto her husband, and said, Send me, I pray thee, one of the young men, and one of the asses, that I may run to the man of God, and come again.

"And he said, Wherefore wilt thou go to him to day? it is neither new moon, nor sabbath. And she said, It shall be well" (vv. 22,23).

Please notice that the woman said, "It <u>shall</u> be well." It wasn't well yet, because her child was still dead.

We need to watch the confession of our mouths. Proverbs 4:23 says, "Keep thy heart with all diligence; for out of it are the issues of life."

"Then she saddled an ass, and said to her servant, Drive, and go forward; slack not thy riding for me, except I bid thee.

"So she went and came unto the man of God to mount Carmel. And it came to pass, when the man of God saw her afar off, that he said to Gehazi his servant, Behold, yonder is that Shunammite:

"Run now, I pray thee, to meet her, and say unto her, Is it well with thee? is it well with thy husband? is it well with the child? And she answered, It is well.

"And when she came to the man of God to the hill, she caught him by the feet: but Gehazi came near to thrust her away. And the man of God said, Let her alone; for her soul is vexed within her: and the Lord hath hid it from me, and hath not told me.

"Then she said, Did I desire a son of my Lord? did I not say, Do not deceive me?

"Then he said to Gehazi, Gird up thy loins, and take my staff in thine hand, and go thy way: if thou meet any man, salute him not; and if any salute thee, answer him not again: and lay my staff upon the face of the child.

"And the mother of the child said, As the Lord liveth, and as thy soul liveth, I will not leave thee. And he arose, and followed her.

"And Gehazi passed on before them, and laid the staff upon the face of the child; but there was neither voice, nor hearing. Wherefore he went again to meet him, and told him, saying, The child is not awaked" (2 Kings 4:24–31).

Witness that Elisha said, "Is it well with thee?"

She said, "It is well."

He said, "Is it well with thy husband?"

She said, "It is well."

He said, "Is it well with thy son?"

She said, "All is well." Yet her son was dead, lying at home.

The Shunammite woman went to meet the man of God with an expectant spirit. The atmosphere of expectancy is the breeding ground of miracles.

**She was about to make a withdrawal
on the deposit she had made into
Elisha, the prophet of God.**

It Is Well

There is a story told of a succesful presbyterian businessman from Chicago named Horatio G. Spafford who was also a noted Gospel musician.

However, tragedy struck during the great Chicago fire of 1871. Some months prior, Mr. Spafford had secured great investments in real estate which were completely abolished during this disaster.

"Desiring a rest for his wife and four daughters as well as wishing to assist D.L. Moody and Sankey in one of their campaigns in Great Britain, Spafford planned a European trip for his family in November of 1873. Due to unexpected last minute business developments, he had to remain in Chicago, but he sent his wife and four daughters on ahead as scheduled on the S.S. *Ville du Havre*. He expected to follow in a few days.

"On November 22 the ship was struck by the *Lochearn*, an English vessel, and sank in twelve minutes. Several days later the survivors were finally landed at Cardiff, Wales, and Mrs. Spafford cabled her husband, 'Saved alone.'

"Shortly afterward Spafford left by ship to join his bereaved wife. It is thought that on the sea near the area where his four daughters drowned, Spafford penned this test whose words so significantly discribe his own personal grief."

"When peace like a river, attendeth my way, When sorrows like sea billows roll. Whatever my lot, Thou hast taught me to say, It is well, it is well with my soul."[1]

Something told this little Shunnamite woman that if she could just get to the man of God, everything would be all right. Something was about to happen.

The Spirit of the Lord revealed to Elisha that there was something wrong with the boy. He told his servant Gehazi, to take his staff and and lay it upon him.

He took his staff, laid it on the boy, however, nothing happened. He brought back the report that the child was still dead.

Personal Contact

Sometimes your miracle needs personal contact. Sometimes the intern can't fix what a well–experienced doctor can. Sometimes we don't need a healing line, we need the personal touch of the Master, Jesus Christ.

Kathleen from Tulsa, Oklahoma needed a touch from the Master. When the Lord led her to request a prayer cloth from our Breakthrough ministry, she had no idea she would find a lump on her breast a short time later. When she received the prayer cloth, she immediately claimed her healing and pinned the cloth to her clothing. The lump was gone within days!

The Shunammite woman demanded personal contact from Elisha. Why? Perhaps she discerned that his servant, Gehazi, was a petty thief and a hypocrite. For later,

Elisha would discover him trying to swindle Namaan, the leper, of his clothes and money. (See 2 Kings 5:21–27.)

Regardless, this woman was not leaving until she received her son again to life.

"And when Elisha was come into the house, behold, the child was dead, and laid upon his bed. He went in therefore, and shut the door upon them twain, and prayed unto the Lord.

"And he went up, and lay upon the child, and put his mouth upon his mouth, and his eyes upon his eyes, and his hands upon his hands: and he stretched himself upon the child; and the flesh of the child waxed warm.

"Then he returned, and walked in the house to and fro; and went up, and stretched himself upon him: and the child sneezed seven times, and the child opened his eyes.

"And he called Gehazi, and said, Call this Shunammite. So he called her. And when she was come in unto him, he said, Take up thy son" (2 Kings 4:32–36).

Have you ever had a miracle die? This woman's miracle child died, and she took him and laid him on the bed of Elisha.

Elisha went up and lay upon the child and put his mouth upon his mouth, and his eyes upon his eyes, and his hands upon his hands, and he stretched himself upon the child. However, he was just getting warm.

Then the Bible says, Elisha laid on him again. He was not about to give up and let this promised son die. The child then sneezed seven times—seven, the number of God—and opened his eyes.

Without the Lord and His anointing upon your situation, things would surely be hopeless.

I believe the book of Hebrews pays tribute to this steadfast mother and her faith, "Women received their dead raised to life again" (Hebrews 11:35).

Possibly you feel as though the devil has tried to move you out. He has attempted to trick you. He worked to get you to run off and leave your dream. Possibly he told you there wasn't a place for you.

There comes a time in your life when enough is enough. There comes a time when you must draw a line in the spiritual sand and tell the devil you are taking back what rightfully belongs to you.

Now is the time to lift your hands and allow God's anointing to come upon you. With the same faith of this steadfast mother, don't allow yourself to be left out of the blessing of God for your life.

3

The Social Outcast

*When she had heard of Jesus, came in the
press behind, and touched his garment.
For she said, If I may touch but his clothes,
I shall be whole (Mark 5:27,28).*

Several years ago, I attended a conference with my
late pastor and mentor, Dr. Lester Sumrall, at the the Oral
Roberts University Mabee Center in Tulsa, Oklahoma.
There were approximately 8,000 men and women in
attendance.

We were seated on two folding chairs next to the cur-
tain near the front of the platform. I don't remember who
the guest speaker was that particular evening but the
events that transpired in the next few moments made an
impact on my life forever.

Brother Sumrall reached over and put his hand on my
knee, and he put his other hand on his belly, and he said,
"Do you feel that?"

I had to confess that I did. It was as though something was leaping on the inside of my belly. Dr. Sumrall
said, "That's the healing anointing. Dr. Oral Roberts is
somewhere in this building."

I said, "Pastor, he's scheduled to be out of the state. He's not here."

Then he squeezed my knee to let me know that he was trying to teach me something. He said, "It doesn't matter to me where they say he is. My spirit tells me that anointing is here."

At that moment, a hand squeezed the back of my neck and shook hands with my pastor. Dr. Oral Roberts proceeded to walk to the platform, interrupt the speaker, and said, "The healing anointing is here."

I believe even as you read this book the anointing is available where you are to heal, deliver and restore whatever is broken in your life or in your family!

The Lord is Passing By

There is the story of a woman who was an outcast for twelve years. It is the narrative of a social misfit who wasn't even allowed to be with her family or friends. The Gospel of Mark records it this way:

"And Jesus went with him; and much people followed him, and thronged him.

"And a certain woman, which had an issue of blood twelve years, And had suffered many things of many physicians, and had spent all that she had, and was nothing bettered, but rather grew worse, when she had heard of Jesus, came in the press behind, and touched his garment. For she said, If I may touch but his clothes, I shall be whole.

"And straightway the fountain of her blood was dried up; and she felt in her body that she was healed of that plague.

"And Jesus, immediately knowing in himself that virtue had gone out of him, turned him about in the press, and said, Who touched my clothes?

"And his disciples said unto him, Thou seest the multitude thronging thee, and sayest thou, Who touched me? And he looked round about to see her that had done this thing.

"But the woman fearing and trembling, knowing what was done in her, came and fell down before him, and told him all the truth.

"And he said unto her, Daughter, thy faith hath made thee whole; go in peace, and be whole of thy plague" (5:24–34).

Jesus was traveling from place to place ministering to the needs of the people. Before entering this town he had been to the other side of Galilee casting out a legion of devils from a man who was possessed. Today, however, Jesus was on His way to Jairus' house, a ruler of the synagogue, to minister to a sick child.

In route, a crowd gathered around Him. He could barely move. Women lifted their children up to try to get a glimpse of Jesus. Strong men tried to push their way through the crowd, so that their eyes could meet His.

I've heard St. Augustine once said, "Flesh presses, but faith touches." People today are no different. Some seek Jesus because they are curious. Some are simply among the crowd because they are looking to see somebody else. But God knows the difference.

Jesus never looks upon a gathering of people as a mob. He knows each person in a crowd intimately and personally.

There are those who can look Him in the eye and never truly see Him. Some may touch His clothes, and yet never feel Him. There are those who can listen to the articulation of His voice but never really hear Him.

On this day, however, travel with me to the city upon a hill. It's a swelteringly hot day. The Palestinian sun is beating down on the cobblestone streets of Jerusalem. There's a large crowd gathered. Dust is everywhere. Jesus is passing by.

Some declare, "He's a prophet." Others say, "He's a madman." One man said, "All I know is that I was blind, and now I see."

Good news traveled swiftly. It rang in the ears of blind Bartimaeus. He heard that Jesus was passing by. Zaccheus climbed up in a sycamore tree, because he heard that Jesus was passing by.

This day, allow me to draw your attention to the woman in the Gospel of Mark whose story you just read. She was not someone who decided to show up in the crowd to see what the Master would do for someone else. She did not come to be a cheerleader at another person's miracle. She did not even come to be seen. She came in the press behind.

History bears out that this woman was a social outcast. It reveals that possibly she was abused, or perhaps just promiscuous. Whatever the situation, she could have said to herself, "I'm to blame for my condition."

She was tired. The stench on that hot day was permeating the atmosphere around her. People were screaming out, "Unclean!"

According to Hebrew law, she was not permitted to touch another person. For twelve years she was excommunicated from the fellowship of the saints. By law, she was separated from her husband and children. For twelve lonely years she suffered the stigma of living just out of reach—and out of touch—of another person.

It had been twelve years since anyone had brushed her hair back from her face. It had been twelve years since she felt the warmth of a handshake, or the love of an embrace. She had spent everything she had just to try to rid herself of the debilitating disease that had kept her all alone.

Now this woman was thin and emaciated from the slow toll this disease had taken upon her. But she had heard other testimonies of how Jesus healed and faith began to spring up within her.

There may come a time when you will give anything for one moment's relief from your pain. This woman knew that feeling, and she needed hope beyond the scope of human limitation.

The News of Jesus' Miracles

There were four things this woman did in this narrative. First she heard Jesus was in town. This woman had possibly heard the stories of the multitudes Jesus had healed from town to town. Perhaps she heard that Jesus had healed the man with the withered hand. (Mark 3.) Maybe one of her relatives shared with her the wonderful display of compassion Jesus had toward the widow of Nain whose son had died, but was raised back to life again. (Luke 7.) Something so stirred her to the very depths of her spirit to believe this man, the carpenter's son, could heal her also.

Can you see this little woman bent over? She heard the good news that Jesus was passing by. She had a decision to make. She could discard her faith and give up, or she could direct her faith and be lifted up.

She had a choice to make. She could let her mountain move her faith, or she could let her faith move her mountain. She determined that she not only had faith, but she had <u>faith to pursue</u>.

You see, the proof of desire is in pursuit. If you want your miracle badly enough, there's nothing that can stand in your way.

If you desire the Master's touch, it doesn't matter what anyone says about you, nor does it matter what people think about you.

So with dogged determination, declare within yourself, "I don't care what anyone else thinks, I have to get to Jesus!" There isn't anyone else who can help you out of your situation.

She Spoke to Herself

Second, she spoke to herself. She said within herself, "If I can but touch the hem of His garment, I know I will be made whole."

Faith will cause you to talk to yourself. There are two hinges to your faith found in Romans chapter 10 and verse 10 which says, "For with the heart man believeth unto righteousness; and with the mouth confession is made unto salvation."

Countless others experienced this Man's touch, whose face was weather–beaten and whose hands were calloused. Mark 6:53–56 reveal,

"And when they had passed over, they came into the land of Gennesaret, and drew to the shore. And when they were come out of the ship, straightway they knew him, And ran through that whole region round about, and began to carry about in beds those that were sick, where they heard he was.

"And whithersoever he entered, into villages, or cities, or country, they laid the sick in the streets, and besought him that they might touch if it were but the border of his garment: and as many as touched him were made whole."

You don't need another preacher. You need Jesus. Your family doesn't need another doctor. They need Jesus. Your friend doesn't need another counselor. They need Jesus' healing, delivering and saving touch.

This woman, whose body was afflicted with an issue of blood, began to say within herself—or she began to rehearse within her spirit—words of faith.

Humility and embarrassment demanded that she share it with no one. She was wrapped and draped in rags and hiding behind the crowd. She extended her bony little fingers, with eyes sunken in her head, just to touch the hem of His garment.

There are some things you just can't talk to anyone-about. Her situation couldn't shared with anyone.

**God wants to set every person free
from the very thing that they cannot
share with another soul.**

Perhaps you are that person.

I am not referring to the testimony you tell everyone. I am talking about that thing that you can't tell anyone, possibly not even your family. I am talking about that thing that makes you walk the floor at night. I am talking about that thing you can't even share with your pastor.

As this woman began to talk inside herself, it was as though a painter was beginning to paint a picture on the canvas of her soul. The longer she continued to rehearse in her spirit, the clearer the image became.

This is what happens on the inside of you when you begin to say, "If I can just touch Him, I know I'll be made whole."

You can't see it, and at first it doesn't seem real. In the beginning, you don't think it's ever going to happen, but you just keep speaking to yourself. And, the more you say it, the more the Holy Spirit anoints it. On the canvas of your life, God takes His Word and begins to paint an image of you delivered, healed and set free!

Let me share with you this example. The prophet Jeremiah saw something out of the ordinary.

"Moreover the word of the Lord came unto me, saying, Jeremiah, what seest thou? And I said, I see a rod of an almond tree. Then said the Lord unto me, Thou hast well seen: for I will hasten my word to perform it" (Jeremiah 1:11,12).

We have apple orchards around Columbus, Ohio. On January 13th, the day I was born, there was 27 inches of snow on the ground as far as the eye could see. Wouldn't it be a strange thing to see one apple tree in the middle of an orchard hanging full of bright red apples in the middle of the winter?

What was God saying in this passage of Scripture? First, let me point out what the Hebrew writer said, "By him therefore let us offer the sacrifice of praise to God continually, that is, the fruit of our lips giving thanks to his name" (13:15).

Don't think God has forsaken you in the middle of your winter—the tragedy of your life. Stand your ground.

In Jeremiah and Hebrews, our Heavenly Father is saying, "In the middle of the winter of your life, lift up your head, lift up your hands and from a heart filled with faith, begin to declare, 'I shall be made whole.'" The fruit of your lips will be the attraction, and the Lord will hasten to perform His Word.

Let me share an illustration. The woman with the issue of blood did not have her healing yet for she said "I shall be made whole." Mark 11:22–24 declares,

"And Jesus answering saith unto them, Have faith in God. For verily I say unto you, That whosoever shall say unto this mountain, Be thou removed, and be thou cast into the sea; and shall not doubt in his heart, but shall believe that those things which he saith shall come to pass; he shall have whatsoever he saith.

"Therefore I say unto you, What things soever ye desire, when ye pray, believe that ye receive them, and ye shall have them."

What can the devil do with you when he comes and says, "You don't have your healing," and you respond, "I shall!"

He may say, "Your marriage is a mess." You answer, "But I shall have restoration."

If you are bound by addiction, you know you shall be set free. The devil can't do anything when somebody has their faith zeroed in on the "I shall have it!"

Faith Touched Him

The third thing this woman did was touch the hem of His garment. The definition of "touch" in this Scripture is the Greek word "hapto" which means "to take hold of."[2] She did not just brush by Jesus. This woman took hold of God with tenacity.

They tried to beat her away, but she grabbed that purple thread in the bottom of His garment, because she understood transference. He became her scapegoat.

According to Hebrew law, one goat was killed on the day of atonement, but there was another called the scapegoat. The priest took his hands and dipped them in blood, and put the blood on the scapegoat. The Bible records that the animal was then taken out into an uninhabited place and released to bear the burden of Israel's sins.

This woman wasn't just trying to receive something from Jesus. She had something on her that she wanted to put on Him—a life ravaging disease.

Isaiah 53:4,5 says, "Surely he hath borne our griefs, and carried our sorrows: yet we did esteem him stricken, smitten of God, and afflicted.

"But he was wounded for our transgressions, he was bruised for our iniquities: the chastisement of our peace was upon him; and with his stripes we are healed."

She Felt Healing Power

Finally, this woman with the issue of blood felt healing come in and sickness go out! Once she touched the border of Jesus' garment, she was immediately set free. How wonderful one touch can be!

Once this woman received her healing, she had hoped to slip back into the crowd and be on her way. However, Jesus called her out after she admitted to touching Him. "And he said unto her, Daughter, thy faith hath made thee whole; go in peace, and be whole of thy plague" (Mark 5:34).

Jesus didn't just heal this woman, he restored her from the stigma of being a social outcast. This woman was still excommunicated from the temple, still separated from her husband, still ostracized by her friends. However, Jesus adopted her as one of His own.

"According as he hath chosen us in him before the foundation of the world, that we should be holy and without blame before him in love:

"Having predestinated us unto the adoption of children by Jesus Christ to himself, according to the good pleasure of his will, to the praise of the glory of his grace, wherein he hath made us accepted in the beloved.

"In whom we have redemption through his blood, the forgiveness of sins, according to the riches of his grace" (Ephesians 1:4–7).

New life began for this woman both physically and spiritually! She no longer had to stand off at a distance. She was now God's child!

Delivered by God's Power

Not long ago, the parents of a backslidden daughter, named Chrissy, wrote to our ministry requesting a prayer cloth.

This young woman had been running from the Lord and was deep into the partying, drugs and alcohol scene. Her only friends were those steeped in this same lifestyle.

After receiving the prayer cloth, Chrissy's parents placed the cloth on a photo of her, and began to see immediate results.

Her brother begged her to attend a revival service with him. However, when she arrived the revival was over. The devil had convinced her that she was so bad, she just couldn't change.

Everyone in town talked about her. But one day she attended another service in which the pastor ministered about the Samaritan woman. It was as though the pastor was talking directly to her, and she felt the power of God break the bondage of Satan in her life.

Two months after Chrissy's parents placed the cloth on her picture, she was back home, serving the Lord!

Reach Out and Touch the Lord

Let me share with you this final word from Luke chapter 16, verse 16, which declares, "The law and the prophets were until John. Since that time, the kingdom of God is preached, and every man presseth into it."

Oh, my dear friend, this is the day and this is the hour when we will no longer have to wait for a shadow to touch and heal us. We can each personally receive whatever it is we need from Jesus!

Like the woman with the issue of blood,

We must press forward, press in and press through until we reach Jesus and take hold of His miracle–working power.

We may be buffeted and beaten back but we must not turn away!

With Jesus on his way to heal a sick child, this woman could have said, "My problem is too small compared to Jairus' daughter. She's already on her death bed. Perhaps I shouldn't trouble the Master." There is more than enough healing available for you.

There is that touch that makes a demand on His anointing. There is that touch that will not let go. There is that wrestling that says, "You cannot go until you bless me."

Jesus wants you to cast all of your cares on Him. Touch Him and let it go. He's passing by this moment with a tangible anointing. I love that old song which says,

Reach out and touch the Lord as He goes by. You will find He's not too busy to hear your heart's cry. He is passing by this moment your needs to supply. Reach out and touch the Lord as He goes by.[5]

You've prayed long enough, hoped long enough and believed long enough. Today is your day. The Bible says,

"(For he saith, I have heard thee in a time accepted, and in the day of salvation have I succoured thee: behold, now is the accepted time; behold, now is the day of salvation)" (2 Corinthians 6:2).

Can you sense His presence? He is not a ghostly being far removed from you. He is with you right now as you read this book!

You don't have to be lost in this crowd. Jesus is passing by! Reach out and touch Him!

4

THE ONLY CHILD

My little daughter lieth at the point of
death: I pray thee, come and lay thy
hands on her, that she may be healed;
and she shall live (Mark 5:23).

Jesus had just arrived back in the city of Capernaum after a short ministry trip to the country of the Gadarenes. While there, he cast a legion of demons from a man who dwelt among the caves. (See Mark 5:1–20.) This was not the first time he had commanded the devil to free a possessed person.

Jesus was about to resume His Father's work in the home town of Peter, Andrew, James, John, and Matthew. It was here that he would confront the sting of death.

This city was the location of more miracles than any other in the world. It was to this place that the multitudes brought their sick and feeble. It was to this site that the diseased were laid at Jesus' feet.

This was the metropolis where the blind received their sight, beholding the wonderful face of their Savior; the deaf heard the sound of Jesus' voice for the first time; the limbs of lame men and women were straightened; the mentally insane were returned to their right mind; epileptics were arrested from the seizures which had stricken their bodies; the possessed were unloosed from the confines of the devil's bondage and the chains of sin that were binding prostitutes and tax collectors were broken by the anointing. But the climatic miracle was about to occur—the resurrection of the dead.

"And when Jesus was passed over again by ship unto the other side, much people gathered unto him: and he was nigh unto the sea.

"And, behold, there cometh one of the rulers of the synagogue, Jairus by name; and when he saw him, he fell at his feet, And besought him greatly, saying, My little daughter lieth at the point of death: I pray thee, come and lay thy hands on her, that she may be healed; and she shall live.

"And Jesus went with him; and much people followed him, and thronged him" (Mark 5:21–24).

He Will Awaken

As we see from this passage of Scripture, Jairus was a ruler of one of the synagogues. However, with tremendous reverence and humility, though a religious leader, *he fell at Jesus' feet.*

Jairus came personally to Jesus amidst the crowd to beg Him fervently to cure his only daughter. He bid Him come and lay his hands upon her and rescue her from the victory of the grave. Just as the centurion honored Jesus as a man in authority (Matthew 8:5–13.), so Jairus esteemed Him as one greater than himself.

For he knew that nowhere else could he obtain the mercy and miracle he so desperately needed.

He needed just one touch of the anointing.

At this juncture, I think it is important to note that the name Jairus means, "he will awaken."

Names during Biblical times held great significance or importance for the person to whom it belonged. When Paul said, referring to Jesus, "Thou art the Christ" (Matthew 16:16a). He meant Jesus was the anointed one whose breaks every yoke. Can you imagine Jairus' mother the day he was born? Possibly he aroused her soul and, the joy of his birth, awakened her to new life.

This day, however, death had darkened Jairus' heart and deprived him of the honor of his name. Despondency of spirit over his dying daughter drove him to desperation.

George Eliot once said, "There is no despair so absolute as that which comes with the first moments of our first great sorrow, when we have not yet known what it is to have suffered and be healed, to have despaired and recovered hope." [1]

Jairus was a desperate man in search of drastic measures. However, God was preparing his heart, through a seemingly insignificant series of events, to receive his child to life again.

An Interruption

Jairus ran all the way from his home to meet the Master. His twelve–year–old daughter was lying at home dying. He didn't have time for church. He needed a miracle. He didn't have time for a theological discourse. His daughter needed touched by the anointing.

Jairus was in a hurry and, all of a sudden, Jesus stopped in mid–step. Can you imagine how Jarius felt?

Out of nowhere Jesus said, "Who touched me?" (This refers, of course, to the story from the previous chapter of how the woman with the issue of blood was healed.)

Jesus passed through the throng to the house of Jairus, to raise the ruler's daughter from the dead. But in His goodness He performed another miracle along the way. There was enough anointing to heal both the woman with the issue of blood and Jairus' daughter.

I like to say that the anointing is like a fragrance which attracts the blessing and favor of God. Jesus' anointing not only reached its ordained target, but enriched the air around Him. Virtue flowed from Jesus, as a sweet smelling aroma from spring flowers.

Jesus is always ready to heal the sick and deliver the oppressed, so do not hesitate to put yourself in His path. The anointing is bountiful, and it only takes one touch.

Why was this woman's story important to Jairus? Jesus didn't stop and ask the question, "Who touched me?" because He didn't know who had touched Him.

It was that little woman—the social outcast. She didn't know anything about church. In fact, her issue of blood may have been caused by a sexually transmitted disease. She had been ostracized from society for twelve years, separated from her husband according to the law, and excommunicated from the fellowship of the saints. For twelve long and lonely years, she walked the streets with people yelling, "Unclean!" at her.

But she thought, "I'll just slip in. I'll get my blessing and run." However, Jesus demanded, "Who touched me?" His disciples laughed and said, "Everybody's touching you." But Jesus responded, "Someone touched me differently, because I perceive that virtue has gone out of Me."

What is virtue? It is power. Virtue is the anointing that will break every yoke of bondage. (Isaiah 10:27.) It is the power to propel you through every line of Satan's defense!

Just moments earlier, this woman was unclean and bleeding. The stench was sickening, but one touch from the Anointed One changed all of that.

Have you ever wondered why Jesus didn't proceed directly to Jairus' house? After all, the woman had received her healing, and she he didn't want any attention drawn to herself anyway.

Why didn't Jesus just go on?

**Jesus wanted Jairus to witness
the miraculous.**

I think Jesus must have detected just a little doubt in Jairus' heart, so He stopped. Then (to paraphrase) Jesus turned to the woman with the issue of blood and said, "Come here, little lady, and testify."

All of a sudden this little woman began to share the tragedy and trials of her life. She began to confess how for twelve long, lonely years no one wanted to touch her. But this day she didn't come to be touched by someone, but rather, to touch Someone.

I can almost see the look of anxiety and impatience upon Jairus' face. All of a sudden, while Jesus was ministering to that woman, some of Jairus' servants came with a bad report.

Your Only Child is Dead

"While he yet spake, there came from the ruler of the synagogue's house certain which said, Thy daughter is dead: why troublest thou the Master any further?" (Mark 5:35).

A few people came and told Jairus, "Don't trouble Him any longer. It's over. Your girl is dead."

But then Jairus began to hear that little woman testify, and every time she would say, "for twelve years," something would begin to leap inside of him.

I think Jairus began to remember, "The moment this woman moved under the darkness of exile was the morning my dream child dawned like the breaking of a new day. My little girl was born, she fulfilled the totality of my name, and my soul was awakened.

"For twelve years this woman has trudged through life with everything going wrong, and for twelve years I have experienced joy unspeakable and full of glory. I have known the warmth of my daughter's hugs and the sweetness of her kisses."

Then Jairus heard this woman say, "When I touched Him, I was made whole."

Friend, you don't need a preacher. You just need Jesus. You don't need another healing service. You just need to touch the hem of His garment!

Her Testimony Was His Triumph

Jesus made the woman with the issue of blood testify for three reasons. First, through her confession, this woman would have to come into direct relationship with Him. For too long, the body of Christ has just wanted to grab a blessing and run away while Jesus is longing for a relationship.

The book of Romans declares, "That if thou shalt confess with thy mouth the Lord Jesus, and shalt believe in thine heart that God hath raised him from the dead, thou shalt be saved. For with the heart man believeth unto righteousness; and with the mouth confession is made unto salvation" (10:9,10).

The second reason this woman needed to testify about her miracle was because Jairus' faith needed strengthened. Romans 10:17 says, "So then faith cometh by hearing, and hearing by the word of God."

Jairus needed to know that if Jesus could heal her, He could surely heal his daughter.

Finally, Jesus made her testify because He wanted to glorify the Father through her miracle. The Bible also states the importance of testifying to the miracle–working power of Jesus, "And they overcame him by the blood of the Lamb, and by the word of their testimony; and they loved not their lives unto the death" (Revelation 12:11).

Only Believe

"As soon as Jesus heard the word that was spoken, he saith unto the ruler of the synagogue, Be not afraid, only believe" (Mark 5:36).

Oswald Chambers once said, "Death cancels everything but truth."[4]

**Jesus will hold you when your world
seems to be crashing around you.**

Take this testimony for example:

Walter and Nancy were believing for a healing for their son, Joey. Not long ago they wrote to our ministry:

"Joey is ten years old and watches Breakthrough faithfully every day. Joey was born three months premature and, as a result, has a condition called cerebral palsy. He is currently in a wheelchair. His prayer is that the Lord will heal him completely.

"A few years ago, friends attended Dominion Camp Meeting. They brought back a prayer cloth and placed it on Joey.

"A few weeks later, we noticed the one leg that was shorter than the other had grown. It grew so much that the shoe lift he had was taken down by several inches.

"Our prayer and Joey's prayer is for a complete and total healing so he will never have to be in a wheelchair again."

Jesus only asked one thing of Jairus—that he believe. Isaiah 41:10 says, "Fear thou not; for I am with thee: be not dismayed; for I am thy God: I will strengthen thee; yea, I will help thee; yea, I will uphold thee with the right hand of my righteousness."

She is Only Asleep

"And he suffered no man to follow him, save Peter, and James, and John the brother of James. And he cometh to the house of the ruler of the synagogue, and seeth the tumult, and them that wept and wailed greatly.

"And when he was come in, he saith unto them, Why make ye this ado, and weep? the damsel is not dead, but sleepeth. And they laughed him to scorn. But when he had put them all out, he taketh the father and the mother of the damsel, and them that were with him, and entereth in where the damsel was lying" (Mark 5: 37–40).

Jesus took no one with Him into the room of the child except the father, mother, Peter, James and John.

It was the custom of the Jewish people to mourn the dead for seven days. During this time, they blew a pipe which produced a loud, ear–piercingly shrill sound that mixed with the cries of the mourners.

When Jesus arrived and announced that the child was only asleep, the Bible says, "They laughed Him to scorn." This is a poor translation; in essence, they ridiculed Him for such a ludicrous statement.

"And he took the damsel by the hand, and said unto her, Talitha cumi; which is, being interpreted, Damsel, I say unto thee, arise.

"And straightway the damsel arose, and walked; for she was of the age of twelve years. And they were astonished with a great astonishment" (vv. 41,42).

Think of the Jesus' compassion when He raised Jairus' daughter and returned her to her father's delicate care.

I can only imagine Jesus gazing into this child's eyes, after commanding her to come back from the door of death, and saying, "Little lamb, sit up." With the devotion of a shepherd, He brought back the one lamb whom the wolves had taken from among the other ninety–nine. He ushered her back into the sheepfold.

The glory of the resurrection of Jairus' daughter illuminated his soul. I can almost hear the words of the Psalmist ringing in his ears, "Thy word is a lamp unto my feet, and a light unto my path" (119:105). Jairus was once again able to live up to the honor of his name, "he awakens."

The Anointing is Available for You

Maybe you are at the end of yourself. Possibly you have power and prestige but your promised child lies at home battling a debilitating disease.

Perhaps you have spent everything you have, and nothing in your life is any better. Perchance you have tried everything else. Possibly you have attempted even the most experimental procedures to fight sickness, and nothing has worked. Right now, at this very moment, I believe "now faith" is building on the inside of you.

**Hope is being painted, like a fresh
anointing, to believe the unbelievable
and receive the unimaginable.**

You don't need another doctor, you need Jesus. You don't need a better psychiatrist, you need Jesus. You don't need more counseling, you need Jesus.

The anointing is available to save you, cleanse you, heal you and set you free. But, if your faith is still in need of encouragement and strength, read on. . . your miracle is surely on the way!

5

THE DESPERATE FATHER

But if thou canst do any thing,
have compassion on us, and help us.
Jesus said unto him, If thou canst believe,
all things are possible to him
that believeth (Mark 9:22b,23).

All throughout the news we are hearing that people
in the United States are going back to church. I am thank-
ful and happy that we are returning to the faith of our
founding fathers; however, I am a little concerned about
what the people are going to receive when they get there.

Will they receive the dead rigors of religion? Will
they receive the cadencing creeds of men? Will they hear
the doctrines of men?

Or, instead, will they see a display that outstrips
human ability and gives hope beyond the scope of human
limitation? Will they witness a power—the anointing—
which will put them in contact with the reality of a resurrected Christ who broke the bands of wickedness and slew
death and resurrected itself from the dead? This is the
same anointing which gives power to as many as will call
upon His name.

Unfortunately, America and the world are held hostage! Their captor is not a terrorist organization or a political dictator. Rather, it is the deceptive devices of the alien armies of the Antichrist that assail the minds of unsuspecting believers.

Believers and sinners alike pose such questions as "Can God still heal and deliver?"

If It Be Thy Will

Throughout the Bible, there are only three major questions concerning the healing and delivering anointing of Jesus Christ, the Anointed One. The first question some ask is, "If it be thy will."

"And there came a leper to him, beseeching him, and kneeling down to him, and saying unto him, If thou wilt, thou canst make me clean.

"And Jesus, moved with compassion, put forth his hand, and touched him, and saith unto him, I will; be thou clean. And as soon as he had spoken, immediately the leprosy departed from him, and he was cleansed" (Mark 1:40–42).

If it were really God's will to heal and deliver one person and not the other, I believe that there would be at least one instance proving this in the Bible. However, God's response to this leper was a resounding, "I will!"

I don't know what you have been told, but I know this. Healing and deliverance are not promises; they are facts. Therefore, if God didn't want to heal or deliver you, He shouldn't have.

Isaiah 53:4,5 state, "Surely he hath borne our griefs, and carried our sorrows: yet we did esteem him stricken, smitten of God, and afflicted. But he was wounded for our transgressions, he was bruised for our iniquities: the chastisement of our peace was upon him; and with his stripes we are healed."

Will You Be Healed?

The second question concerning healing and deliverance is, "Will you be made whole?"

The Gospel of John records the story of the man by the pool of Bethesda,

"Now there is at Jerusalem by the sheep market a pool, which is called in the Hebrew tongue Bethesda, having five porches.

"In these lay a great multitude of impotent folk, of blind, halt, withered, waiting for the moving of the water. For an angel went down at a certain season into the pool, and troubled the water: whosoever then first after the troubling of the water stepped in was made whole of whatsoever disease he had.

"And a certain man was there, which had an infirmity thirty and eight years. When Jesus saw him lie, and knew that he had been now a long time in that case, he saith unto him, <u>Wilt thou be made whole</u>?

"The impotent man answered him, Sir, I have no man, when the water is troubled, to put me into the pool: but while I am coming, another steppeth down before me. Jesus saith unto him, Rise, take up thy bed, and walk.

"And immediately the man was made whole, and took up his bed, and walked: and on the same day was the sabbath" (5:2–9).

Will you be made whole? Are you tired of the struggle; tired of the pain; tired of the bondage; tired of the infirmity; tired of the darkness; tired of the loneliness; tired of the insecurity; and, tired of the confusion? It's time to reach out and touch the Lord!

Where there is doubt concerning the will of God, faith is strangled and dies. Why?

Faith begins where the will of God is known.

What is the will of God? 3 John 2 says, "Beloved, I wish above all things that thou mayest prosper and be in health, even as thy soul prospereth."

Jesus removed all doubt by performing an indisputable act of authority—by commanding the man to take up his bed and walk.

If Thou Canst
The last question asked regarding healing and deliverance is, "If thou canst . . ." This is the question I want to focus on because the story is so dramatic.

A father had a boy who cast himself into the fire, thrashing and gnawing like a wild man. He came to Jesus and said, "Master, I took my son to your disciples, and they could not heal him."

I believe this father wanted to take his son to Jesus but because He was not in the vicinity he brought him to His disciples instead. The result was fruitless—they could not deliver the child.

There is a nursery rhyme that goes, "Humpty Dumpty sat on a wall. Humpty Dumpty had a great fall. All the king's horses and all the king's men couldn't put Humpty Dumpty back together again."

My question is, "Why do we busy ourselves with the king's horses and the king's men?" We need to take our burdens directly to the King!

A deadening blow had struck at the very heart of this father's natural hope. I believe the failure of the disciples to heal the child was to show that all hope should be directed toward Jesus Christ only. There is an old hymn which says, "My hope is built on nothing less than Jesus' blood and righteousness. I dare not trust the sweetest frame but wholly lean on Jesus' name."[5]

Bring the Boy to Me

I love what Jesus said next to this desperate father, "Bring the boy to me." (See Mark 9:17–19).

"And they brought him unto him: and when he saw him, straightway the spirit tare him; and he fell on the ground, and wallowed foaming.

"And he asked his father, How long is it ago since this came unto him? And he said, Of a child. And ofttimes it hath cast him into the fire, and into the waters, to destroy him: but if thou canst do any thing, have compassion on us, and help us" (vv. 20–22).

Jesus, with blazing eyes, looked into the face of that father and declared as the one who flung the stars into their sockets, "Don't you question what I can do. For it is not a question what I can do, but only what you can believe. For all things are possible to him that believeth." (See v. 23.)

The Bible goes on to say, "When Jesus saw that the people came running together, he rebuked the foul spirit, saying unto him, Thou dumb and deaf spirit, I charge thee, come out of him, and enter no more into him. And the spirit cried, and rent him sore, and came out of him: and he was as one dead; insomuch that many said, He is dead. But Jesus took him by the hand, and lifted him up; and he arose" (vv. 25–27).

Jesus allowed this desperate father to give the prognosis of his child's condition. I believe he wanted the crowd who had gathered to witness the type of miracle that was about to take place.

We need to ask the Lord specifically for what we want. James 4:3 declares, "Ye ask, and receive not, because ye ask amiss, that ye may consume it upon your lusts."

Right in the middle of this father's dissertation, the boy began to have an uncontrollable fit to the point that the onlookers announced, "He is dead."

At that moment, this father had a choice.

**He could discard his faith and give up
or direct his faith and be lifted up.**

The desperateness of this situation gives us keen insight into the greatness of God's mercy for us. Even in the midst of doubting, there was faith as a grain of mustard seed within him to believe.

This man needed a breakthrough. He needed a sudden burst of the advanced knowledge, or revelation, of God, to push him through his surrounding circumstances. There is a time designated by God when His anointing will push you through.

The Anointed One

This desperate father needed to know this man Jesus of Nazareth, the Anointed One. He and his son needed to be touched by the anointing. He needed to know the Christ described in Luke 4.

In this passage, Jesus had just come from the mountain of conflict, where He had been in the presence of God and warred with the devil for 40 days. Afterward, He spoke to the people in the synagogue.

"And he came to Nazareth, where he had been brought up: and, as his custom was, he went into the synagogue on the sabbath day, and stood up for to read. And there was delivered unto him the book of the prophet Esaias. And when he had opened the book, he found the place where it was written,

'The Spirit of the Lord is upon me, because he hath anointed me to preach the gospel to the poor; he hath sent me to heal the brokenhearted, to preach deliverance to the captives, and recovering of sight to the blind, to set at liberty them that are bruised, to preach the acceptable year of the Lord'" (vv.16–19).

Jesus is our jubilee. Jesus is our freedom. Jesus is our great emancipator.

We were slaves to sin and bondage, but now, we are free.

As I shared with you from Luke 4 earlier, Jesus sat down in the synagogue to read from the Torah. History bears out that in every Jewish synagogue there was a special seat. This wasn't just any chair, for it was reserved for the coming Messiah.

Have you ever wondered what Jesus did that made those people so mad that they grabbed Him by the nape of the neck and, took Him to the brow of the hill to throw Him off? He read that passage from the prophet Isaiah, closed that book, and went over and sat down in the seat reserved for the Messiah.

They said, "Who does He think He is?" I think it's very evident who He thought He was. He knew He was that one of whom Isaiah prophesied, "And there shall come forth a rod out of the stem of Jesse, and a Branch shall grow out of his roots: And the spirit of the Lord shall rest upon him, the spirit of wisdom and understanding, the spirit of counsel and might, the spirit of knowledge and of the fear of the Lord" (11:1,2).

Whom Do Men Say That I Am?

During the early days of Jesus' earthly ministry He questioned His disciples as to who men thought He was.

"And they said, Some say that thou art John the Baptist: some, Elias; and others, Jeremias, or one of the prophets. He saith unto them, But whom say ye that I am? And Simon Peter answered and said, Thou art the Christ, the Son of the living God" (Matthew 16:14–16).

The word Christ translated simply means, "the Anointed One who destroys every yoke."

Jesus went on to say, "Blessed art thou, Simon Barjona: for flesh and blood hath not revealed it unto thee, but my Father which is in heaven.

"And I say, also unto thee, That thou art Peter, and upon this rock I will build my church; and the gates of hell shall not prevail against it" (vv. 17,18).

Regardless of what has tried to keep you from the blessing God promised, the gates of hell shall not prevail against you. In other words, God is going to give you a revelation that breaks you through every obstacle Satan has erected.

That is what that father needed whose son cast himself into the fire that I shared with you earlier in this chapter. (See Mark 9). He needed a revelation of who Jesus was!

Authority and Anointing Produce Miracles

The Gospel of John records, "For as the Father hath

life in himself; so hath he given to the Son to have life in himself; And hath given him authority to execute judgment also, because he is the Son of man" (5:26,27).

One translation says He hath given Him authority for and against to execute judgment. Let me say it another way: God has given Jesus authority for us and against the devil to execute judgment. God will judge <u>for</u> you and <u>against</u> the devil.

Because you are "a son of man born into this earth," God has given Jesus Christ power for you and against the devil—because He is <u>the</u> Son of man. He hasn't done this because Jesus is the Son of God.

Jesus Christ, in the power and authority of the Holy Spirit, performed the miraculous among men—not as God, which would not have been miraculous at all, but as a Spirit–anointed man.

Authority in the earth realm comes to you because you have an earth suit—a body. Obviously, to exaggerate the point, you and I are unable to accomplish anything on the earth without a body!

John 4:24 says, "God is a Spirit: and they that worship him must worship him in spirit and in truth." (4:24).

Herein lies the answer to some of the greatest questions that have plagued the minds of men. If God is a loving God, why are babies being aborted? Why are people starving to death? Why are wars and rumors of wars all over the face of the earth? Why is there drug addiction? Why are the hospital beds full?

Let me share this truth with you. Genesis 1:26 says, "And God said, Let us make man in our image, after our likeness: and let them have dominion over the fish of the sea, and over the fowl of the air, and over the cattle, and over all the earth, and over every creeping thing that creepeth upon the earth." God gave us dominion in all the earth.

John 10:1 says, "Verily, verily, I say unto you, He that entereth not by the door into the sheepfold, but climbeth up some other way, the same is a thief and a robber."

Jesus said of Himself, "Verily, verily, I say unto you, I am the door of the sheep" (vs. 7).

What was Jesus talking about in verse 1? He was referring to the devil, the thief. That thief came to steal, kill and destroy. (See John 10:10.) That thief, the devil, came into the earth another way. The devil gained entry into this earth illegally! He is a reprobate, a loser and an intruder! He is here illegally because he has no body.

God, being a Spirit, cannot do anything without a body. This is the reason He said, "The eyes of the Lord run to and fro throughout the whole earth, to shew himself strong in the behalf of all them whose heart is perfected toward him" (2 Chronicles 16:9).

That's why Jesus said, "Be <u>filled</u> with the Spirit." Why didn't He say for the Spirit to get filled with you? Because a Spirit has no authority in this earth.

The authority of having an earth suit gives you the opportunity to manifest miracles, but the anointing gives you the ability to manifest miracles.

Deliverance Has Come

I want to share with you a modern day miracle of a desperate father and mother who reached out in faith to Jesus.

A pastor and his wife sent in a t–shirt to Dominion Camp Meeting believing God to deliver their son from drug addiction. When the t–shirt was returned, the mother ironed it and laid it on her son's bed, in faith, believing her son would come back home.

Two months later Matthew came home and put the t–shirt on. He went out that night to buy some methamphetamines to shoot into his arms. The drug house he usually hung out in had shut down, and all the dealers he knew refused to sell to him, saying their relationship was over. Two months later, Matthew surrendered his life to Jesus.

On Wednesday night of the Raise the Standard Pastors' and Church Workers' Conference, Matthew and his dad were ordained together into the World Harvest Church Ministerial Fellowship.

It was a tremendous night for this pastor because Matthew grew up in institutions, never walked across a platform and never finished high school. To walk across that platform with his son, who now serves in their church, was such an honor. Matthew oversees the praise and worship and the youth ministry for his father, and they are expecting to revolutionize their city.

Jesus walked on the earth at a time much like ours. If there were any less need for Him, He would not have come. Just like the desperate father needed to take desperate measures to see his son delivered, so we must refuse to allow anything to stand in the way of our miracle.

Just as the desperate father questioned, "If thou canst, help us . . ." Jesus looks at you and says, "If thou canst believe, all things are possible to him that believeth" (Mark 9:23).

> **Jesus Christ has discounted every excuse we could offer to stay sick and oppressed.**

He limited Himself to the same power available to us today, the anointing of the Holy Spirit. The Apostle Peter told Cornelius:

"How God anointed Jesus of Nazareth with the Holy Ghost and with power: who went about doing good, and healing all that were oppressed of the devil; for God was with him" (Acts 10:38).

In the final chapter of this book, I am going to illustrate to you from the word of God how you can possess the power and anointing of the Holy Spirit to perform indisputable acts of authority.

6

THE BROKEN MULTITUDES

*(And believers were the more added to the
Lord, multitudes both of men and women.)
Insomuch that they brought forth the sick
into the streets, and laid them on beds and
couches, that at the least the shadow of
Peter passing by might overshadow some
of them (Acts 5:14,15).*

Several years ago, a little girl in our congregation
was dying from an incurable disease. Her parents shared
with my wife, Joni, and said, "We have one of her bed
sheets with us, and we would like Pastor Parsley to pray
over it. After he does, we are going to put it on the bed
and let her sleep on it."

Joni shared this with me during the service. I
wrapped the bed sheet around my shoulders, and I
preached the entire service that way. I gave the sheet back
to that mother and she placed it on her daughter's bed.
Within a week that little girl was completely healed!

This same power and anointing that is beyond anything you could ever comprehend is available to you.
This power goes beyond anything that any electric com-

pany knows anything about. This force is greater than the political machines in operation on this planet. Its impact goes beyond what a doctor can do for you. It will drive you to lift your hands in the valley of your life when everything around you is crumbling.

This supernatural propulsion offers hope when you don't have a dollar to change. It extends hope when the doctors look at you and say you have to die and cannot live. It brings hope in the midst of hopeless situations! You can walk in the anointing of God!

The Tangible Anointing

I remember times when Dr. Lester Sumrall was alive and we would be sitting together in a service. Sometimes he would reach over and pat me on the knee. I would say to myself, "Yes, Lord, I want the anointing that is upon his life."

There is an anointing sufficient enough to break every chain and to destroy every yoke.

I shared with you at the beginning of this book that the anointing is not only tangible, but it is transferrable. What does that mean? Let's look at Pentecostal Headquarters, the Book of Acts.

"And believers were the more added to the Lord, multitudes both of men and women.) Insomuch that they brought forth the sick into the streets, and laid them on beds and couches, that at the least the shadow of Peter passing by might overshadow some of them" (Acts 5:14,15).

After Jesus' resurrection and the subsequent infilling of the Holy Spirit on the day of Pentecost, the church grew dramatically. During one revival service, 5,000 men alone were saved. But great impartation never comes without great persecution.

On several occasions the disciples were beaten and commanded to "no more speak in that name!" (See Acts 4:18.) Still souls were added to the church daily. (Acts 2:47.)

Signs and wonders were so prevalent that many would bring family and friends who were sick, lame, halt, blind, deaf and dumb and lay them in the streets. They watched the way Peter went to temple every day. They knew what time he went and what route he walked, and they said, "If perchance the shadow of Peter might be cast over us, we may be healed."

This didn't have anything to do with Peter's shadow! It was the anointing they sought.

When Peter, full of the Holy Ghost, would walk down the street, his shadow would touch those who were lame, then they would walk; blind, then sight would come into their eyes; deaf, then they would hear; and dumb, then they would speak.

This anointing was also tangible upon the clothing of the Apostle Paul.

"And God wrought special miracles by the hands of Paul: So that from his body were brought unto the sick handkerchiefs or aprons, and the diseases departed from them, and the evil spirits went out of them" (Acts 19:11,12).

I want to begin to see the church walk in the manifested tangible presence of God. Some say those days are over. But I believe:

The Book of Acts will seem like a Sunday school picnic compared to what is going to happen during our lifetime!

The Yoke–Destroying, Burden–Removing Anointing

One of the greatest characteristics of the end–time body of Christ is that we will operate in the spontaneous move of the Holy Spirit because of the anointing upon our lives. The day of personality and persona is over! The time of masquerading pulpiteers is over!

Let me make this announcement: we are not working up to something. We are already in something. We are in the divine flow of almighty God. Isaiah 10:27 says,

"And it shall come to pass in that day, that his burden shall be taken away from off thy shoulder, and his yoke from off thy neck, and the yoke shall be destroyed because of the anointing."

It's the anointing that destroys the yoke! This verse doesn't say that the anointing will break the yoke. It says the anointing will destroy the yoke upon your life. There is a difference between break and destroy. If you break something, it can be repaired. The actual Hebrew translation of the word "destroy" in this verse is to cause to cease to be as if it never existed. I like to refer to it as annihilation. Through the anointing, the forces of light will bombard the forces of darkness that are arrayed against you!

I am not referring to a manmade power! I am not referring to something that will just barely get you by! I am not referring to something that will get you free for a few days and then allow your bondage to come back! I am referring to something that will destroy the yoke of bondage off of your life!

1 John 3:8 declares, "For this purpose the Son of God was manifested, that he might destroy the works of the devil." If Jesus was sent to destroy, or annihilate, the works of the devil, <u>then they are annihilated</u> in your life. The prison door is open but my question to you is, "What are you still doing inside when He has made a way out?" You and I are serving a God who is a way–maker!

Who Is The Lord?

Let's look again at Isaiah 10:27 at the word "yoke," which means the oppression. The word "oppress" means to rule over you.

Whenever sickness, disease or bondage have their tentacles wrapped around your life—then they are lording or ruling over you. I think it's time for anyone (other than

Jesus) who is trying to gain authority over you to recognize who's Lord in your life.

Pharaoh, when addressing Moses about the deliverance of the children of Israel from Egyptian bondage, asked, "Who is the Lord, that I should obey his voice to let Israel go? I know not the Lord, neither will I let Israel go" (Exodus 5:2).

I think it's time for that spirit of infirmity to find out who is Lord. I think it's time for that depression to find out who's really Lord. I think it's time for discouragement to discover just who the Lord is!

The Apostle John wrote, "Little children, keep yourselves from idols" (1 John 5:21).

An idol is anything to which lordship is directed in your life. Lordship refers to a position of authority over you. If there's anything right now that has authority over you, it is my prayer that, before you finish this book, a river of living water will swell up on the inside of you—and that yoke of oppression will be destroyed because of the presence of the anointing.

Let me share with you another testimony of the tangible anointing of the Lord destroying oppression in someone's life.

> Grenada knew the Lord at one time, but had returned to a life of crack and prostitution. Then she started watching Breakthrough and requested a prayer cloth. She awoke one Monday morning alone, burned out on drugs, out of money, out of food and facing eviction. As she laid in her bed in total despair, tired and ready to

die, she heard the mailman. Her prayer cloth had arrived!

She stumbled back to bed, putting the cloth on her head. As she pulled the covers over her head she cried, "God, just let me die!" Within minutes, she was in the bathroom purging both physically and spiritually. She was instantaneously delivered from every addiction that morning. That same week she received a one hundred–fold return on her seed sown into Breakthrough, which was more than enough to pay her bills!

Today, Grenada is back in church and running "The House That Love Built," which ministers to women with similar situations as Grenada's.

Allow me to reiterate: the anointing is tangible. It doesn't matter if it's Moses' face, Elijah's mantle, Elisha's bones, Peter's shadow or Paul's handkerchiefs and aprons. When Grenada came into contact with the anointing on the prayer cloth, only minutes later she was saved, delivered and glorifying God!

The Fragrance of the Anointing

In the Levitical priesthood, there was a ritual of preparing a special holy oil. Poignant herbs were pressed into the oil, making it very aromatic. According to law, this mixture was reserved for the priesthood. When a priest was set apart and anointed, the oil represented a type of the New Testament anointing of the Holy Spirit.

The scent of the anointing oil was distinctive.

If someone was near an Old Testament priest, they could literally smell the anointing upon him. Such an anointing could not be kept a secret.

When the early church was anointed, it was apparent. The Book of Acts records several instances of this. "Then Peter, filled with the Holy Ghost, said unto them . . ." (Acts 4:8). "And they were all filled with the Holy Spirit and spoke the word of God boldly" (4:31b). "Then Saul . . . filled with the Holy Ghost, set his eyes on him" (13:9).

God is still the same. James 1:17 still states, "Every good gift and every perfect gift is from above, and cometh down from the Father of lights, with whom is no variableness, neither shadow of turning." His power and authority through the Holy Spirit have not changed. He is still anointing men and women today.

You can receive the anointing of the Holy Spirit, but you can't hide this phenomenon. Its sweet savor will attract people and blessing to your life.

All Things Are Possible

The anointing of God is a tangible thing; it has substance. Its substance is energy. As I stated earlier in this book, the anointing is a perpetual propulsion of the power of God, which will drive you through every line of Satan's defense.

You have an anointing. You have an unction from God. You have within your being a perpetual propulsion of power from on high. It may need stirred up, but it's in you.

This is a wonderful testimony!

The joys and ecstacy of parenting all too quickly turned into a nightmare as little Betty left the womb of her mother and entered into this world. Her body and limbs were disfigured almost beyond recognition. For 14 long years that little girl lay upon a bed, a hopeless invalid.

Her mother didn't know much about the Bible, but she found part of a verse of Scripture and made it her own. It said, ". . . All things are possible to him that believeth" (Mark 9:23b).

For 14 years, Betty never wore on a piece of clothing. It would not cover her twisted limbs. For 14 years, Betty never had a bite of food cross her tongue. She was fed with a tube into her stomach and intravenously. She had all of her mental faculties and was a bright girl, but day after day she lay at home, never getting any better.

One day her mother came in and said, "Betty, I don't know how you're going to take this, but God showed me part of a Scripture the other day."

Betty interrupted, "Wait a minute, Mama. I had a dream, and in the dream God spoke to me and said, 'All things are possible to him that believeth.' Sunday afternoon is the day I will receive my healing."

Betty's mother said, "That's the verse that God gave me." Then she ran and told her pastor.

Her pastor said, "Well, we don't want to get our hopes up." Why not!? Most people have more hope in an aspirin than they do in our eternal God.

Betty's mother retorted, "God promised my little girl and me that on Sunday afternoon, Jesus is going to heal her body."

So on Sunday afternoon, everyone showed up to see what God was not going to do. They were standing outside looking through the windows. It was documented in all the newspapers.

Betty said, "Mama, I've never worn a dress or had shoes on my feet. Please buy me a dress and shoes. Then, Mama, hang them on the wall where I can see them, because I am going to wear those clothes on Sunday."

On Sunday, a little white cloud appeared in the living room of their home. It moved down the hallway, into Betty's room, and stopped at the end of her bed. She reached out with a little crooked limb and tried to touch it. However, it was just out of reach.

Afterward, her testimony was that God spoke to her in that moment and said, "Always remember, this has nothing to do with Betty Baxter and everything to do with Me."

There comes a time when you can't get your miracle on your own. Try as you will, the heavens seem like brass, and you can't break through.

> That little cloud moved over and touched her body. Witnesses said that they thought her body was coming apart, as her joints began to crack. On that fateful afternoon, every bone in her body became straight.
>
> Betty was completely healed. She put on her dress and shoes. Then she walked around her house with her arms raised in praise to God saying, "All things are possible to him that believeth."[6]

Today Betty is alive and well, preaching the Gospel of Jesus Christ. I want you to know the anointing of God is a tangible energy and it will destroy every yoke in your life! You have something on the inside of you that pushes back the darkness. You have something on the inside of you that dispels the adversary.

You have something bigger than the world on the inside of you. 1 John 4:4 says, "Ye are of God, little children, and have overcome them: because greater is he that is in you, than he that is in the world."

It doesn't matter what may be coming against you. It is the anointing that breaks every yoke.

If you are a born–again believer, the same Jesus that walked the cobblestone streets of Jerusalem, and His anointing, now dwell on the inside of you. The Bible says, "To whom God would make known what is the riches of the glory of this mystery among the Gentiles; which is Christ in you, the hope of glory" (Colossians 1:27).

2 Corinthians 4:7 also refers to the anointing, "But we have this treasure in earthen vessels, that the excellency of the power may be of God, and not of us."

There's something called the anointing of the Holy Ghost living on the inside of you. There's something within you that is bigger than you. It is not only bigger than you, it is bigger than all your problems. God, on the inside of you, is bigger than all your fears and He is bigger than any mountain that you can or cannot see.

John 7:38 said, "He that believeth on me, as the scripture hath said, out of his belly shall flow rivers of living water."

Your spirit becomes the generator that takes the Word of God and changes it into the fuel that the Holy Ghost uses to produce the anointing in your life.

Greater Works

Someone once said, "We don't do the works that Jesus did because we don't do what Jesus did." Let me expound on this thought.

If we have the anointing of the Holy Spirit and His presence in our lives, we should be able to do what Jesus did during His earthly ministry.

But Jesus proclaimed, "Verily, verily, I say unto you, He that believeth on me, the works that I do shall he do also; and greater works than these shall he do; because I go unto my Father.

"And whatsoever ye shall ask in my name, that will I do, that the Father may be glorified in the Son" (John 14:12,13).

Jesus did not perform great miracles because He was the Son of God. Rather, He did exploits through the authority and anointing of the Holy Spirit—as the Son of Man.

Jesus performed miracles for just a few short years in Jerusalem and the surrounding towns. But His disciples and the unending generations after Him performed, and continue to perform, miracles all around the world through the anointing of the Holy Spirit.

You Are Anointed

You are anointed, and if the Lord has ever had His hand on you, He has it on you now! You have an anointing, and that anointing can destroy every yoke!

Our prayer should be, "Lord, give us oil and give us wine." Joel 2:23,24 declare, "Be glad then, ye children of Zion, and rejoice in the Lord your God: for he hath given you the former rain moderately, and he will cause to come down for you the rain, the former rain, and the latter rain in the first month. And the floors shall be full of wheat, and the fats shall overflow with wine and oil."

A dying world is desperately looking to the church for the power to deliver them from its sin–sick state. Through the anointing of the Holy Spirit, we have the answer. God will help us, for He promised He would work with us to confirm His Word. (See Mark 16:20.) And, He will do "exceeding abundantly above all that we ask or think" (Ephesians 3:20a).

We have this hope that, "Beloved, now are we the sons of God, and it doth not yet appear what we shall be: but we know that, when he shall appear, we shall be like him; for we shall see him as he is" (1 John 3:2).

The anointing will make a spiritual warrior and protector out of a backslidden father. The anointing will transform the distraught mother into a powerful intercessor. The anointing will change a calloused teenager into a mighty witness for God. The anointing will transfigure a beaten–down preacher into a blazing prophet!

The last recorded Gospel in the Bible declares, "And there are also many other things which Jesus did, the which, if they should be written every one, I suppose that even the world itself could not contain the books that should be written. Amen" (John 21:25).

EPILOGUE

*Multitudes, multitudes in the valley of
decision: for the day of the Lord is near
in the valley of decision (Joel 3:14).*

This book is full of wonderful stories from not only
the Bible, but also stories of modern day miracles of salvation, healing, and deliverance. However, let me interject this here: you don't have to be born–again to be
healed. Jesus can heal and deliver you anyway.

How sad it would be, though, to live this life in health
and in ease, only to open your eyes on the wrong side of
eternity. There you would be surrounded by the howls
and the cackles in the bowels of the devil's hell, because
you did not have the blessed assurance that Jesus Christ
was your Savior.

Do you know what the Lord has convinced me of?
Tens of thousands of people are in churches across the
country and around the world that want to be saved and
try to act saved, but, sadly, have no assurance that they are
saved. I travel quite a bit, and in every crusade that I con-
duct nearly ninety percent of those in attendance go to
church every Sunday. When I give the altar call, it is

flooded with nearly two–thirds of the entire crowd who then pray the sinner's prayer.

Maybe you are bound by drug addiction, alcohol, self–mutilation, suicidal thoughts, eating disorders or depression. Possibly your body or that of a loved one has been afflicted with cancer, a disability, a terminal illness, migraines or incessant pain. Whatever your situation is, God loves you.

Jesus said, "For God so loved the world, that he gave his only begotten Son, that whosoever believeth in him should not perish, but have everlasting life.

"For God sent not his Son into the world to condemn the world; but that the world through him might be saved" (John 3:16,17).

I'm reminded of the story of a great hymn writer, William Cowper who wrote the beloved song, "There Is A Fountain."

William Cowper was highly respected in English literary circles. However, throughout his life Cowper continued to be plagued by periodic melancholia. Often during these periods he even sought to end his life. It is interesting that some of his most meaningful hymns were written after these times. Till the end of his days Cowper could never completely shake off the belief that God would not turn His back upon him. On his death bed it is said that his face lit up as he uttered these last words, "I am not shut out of heaven after all."[7]

You can rejoice in knowing that you are on your way to heaven with the same confidence that William Cowper had on his deathbed. Romans 10:13 simply states, "For whosoever shall call upon the name of the Lord shall be saved."

At this moment, the Lord has stopped in the midst of your everyday life to deliver you from the clutches of the devil. It doesn't matter what you have done. Heaven is full of thieves, sinners, adulterers and even murderers who have been plunged beneath the fountain of Jesus' crimson blood to wash all their guilty stains.

What if this was your one day to be set free from not only sickness and disease, but also from the terminal disease of sin? What if this was the day you've been waiting on for so long to find a way from under the heavy load of hopelessness and helplessness?

After reading this book, possibly you find yourself ready for a life–changing encounter with Christ, the Anointed One, who takes away the sins of the world. If you have any question in your mind whether or not you are ready to meet God in the next fifteen seconds, I want you to say a prayer with me. At the end of that prayer you will be as sure for heaven as if you were already there.

Are you ready? Don't think about anyone or anything. Just say to yourself, "Am I ready to meet God in the pavilions of glory?" If you answered "no" or "I don't know," pray this prayer:

Heavenly Father, I come to you just like I am. I was born a sinner, and I have committed sins. I ask you to forgive me, wash me in your blood, and give me eternal life.

Satan, you're a liar! I renounce you for you are not my god. Get out of my life!

Lord Jesus Christ, I accept you, believe in you and confess you as my Savior. I will live for you as you show me how. Now let me know I'm on my way to heaven, and I will praise you the rest of my life.

This is the kind of Jesus we serve. He will push His way through every barrier, every bondage and every broken heart just to get to you.

The Gospel of John records, "But as many as received him, to them gave he power to become the sons of God, even to them that believe on his name:

"Which were born, not of blood, nor of the will of the flesh, nor of the will of man, but of God" (1:12,13).

If you prayed this prayer, you are on your way to heaven, and through Jesus Christ's anointing, ready to stand against all the powers of Satan!

ANOINTING SCRIPTURES

And Samuel said unto Jesse, Are here all thy children? And he said, There remaineth yet the youngest, and, behold, he keepeth the sheep. And Samuel said unto Jesse, Send and fetch him: for we will not sit down till he come hither. And he sent, and brought him in. Now he was ruddy, and withal of a beautiful countenance, and goodly to look to. And the Lord said, Arise, anoint him: for this is he. Then Samuel took the horn of oil, and anointed him in the midst of his brethren: and the Spirit of the Lord came upon David from that day forward. So Samuel rose up, and went to Ramah (1 Samuel 16:11–13).

. . . Touch not mine anointed, and do my prophets no harm (1 Chronicles 16:22).

Now know I that the Lord saveth his anointed; he will hear him from his holy heaven with the saving strength of his right hand (Psalm 20:6).

The Lord is my strength and my shield; my heart trusted in him, and I am helped: therefore my heart greatly rejoiceth; and with my song will I praise him. The Lord is their strength, and he is the saving strength of his anointed (Psalm 28:7,8).

Thou lovest righteousness, and hatest wickedness: therefore God, thy God, hath anointed thee with the oil of gladness above thy fellows (Psalm 45:7).

There is a river, the streams whereof shall make glad the city of God, the holy place of the tabernacles of the most High (Psalm 46:4).

Behold, O God our shield, and look upon the face of thine anointed (Psalm 84:9).

But my horn shalt thou exalt like the horn of an unicorn: I shall be anointed with fresh oil (Psalm 92:10).

Behold, I and the children whom the Lord hath given me are for signs and for wonders in Israel from the Lord of hosts, which dwelleth in mount Zion (Isaiah 8:18).

And it shall come to pass in that day, that his burden shall be taken away from off thy shoulder, and his yoke from off thy neck, and the yoke shall be destroyed because of the anointing (Isaiah 10:27).

Who hath believed our report? and to whom is the arm of the Lord revealed? (Isaiah 53:1).

Yea, the Lord will answer and say unto his people, Behold, I will send you corn, and wine, and oil, and ye shall be satisfied therewith: and I will no more make you a reproach among the heathen (Joel 2:19).

And when they had passed over, they came into the land of Gennesaret, and drew to the shore. And when they were come out of the ship, straightway they knew him, And ran through that whole region round about, and began to carry about in beds those that were sick, where they heard he was. And whithersoever he entered, into villages, or cities, or country, they laid the sick in the streets, and besought him that they might touch if it were but the border of his garment: and as many as touched him were made whole (Mark 6:53–56).

Be glad then, ye children of Zion, and rejoice in the Lord your God: for he hath given you the former rain moderately, and he will cause to come down for you the rain, the former rain, and the latter rain in the first month. And the floors shall be full of wheat, and the fats shall overflow with wine and oil. And I will restore to you the years that the locust hath eaten, the cankerworm, and the caterpillar, and the palmerworm, my great army which I sent among you. And ye shall eat in plenty, and be satisfied, and praise the name of the Lord your God, that hath dealt wondrously with you: and my people shall never be ashamed (Joel 2:23–26).

And he said unto them, Go ye into all the world, and preach the gospel to every creature. He that believeth and is baptized shall be saved; but he that believeth not shall be damned. And these signs shall follow them that believe; In my name shall they cast out devils; they shall speak with new tongues; They shall take up serpents; and if they drink any deadly thing, it shall not hurt them; they shall lay hands on the sick, and they shall recover. So then after the Lord had spoken unto them, he was received up into heaven, and sat on the right hand of God. And they went forth, and preached every where, the Lord working with them, and confirming the word with signs following. Amen. (Mark 16:15–20).

The Spirit of the Lord is upon me, because he hath anointed me to preach the gospel to the poor; he hath sent me to heal the brokenhearted, to preach deliverance to the captives, and recovering of sight to the blind, to set at liberty them that are bruised, To preach the acceptableyear of the Lord (Luke 4:18,19).

He that believeth on me, as the scripture hath said, out of his belly shall flow rivers of living water (John 7:38).

Verily, verily, I say unto you, He that believeth on me, the works that I do shall he do also; and greater works than these shall he do; because I go unto my Father. And whatsoever ye shall ask in my name, that will I do, that the Father may be glorified in the Son (John 14:12,13).

(. . . And believers were the more added to the Lord, multitudes both of men and women.) Insomuch that they brought forth the sick into the streets, and laid them on beds and couches, that at the least the shadow of Peter passing by might overshadow some of them (Acts 5:14,15).

How God anointed Jesus of Nazareth with the Holy Ghost and with power: who went about doing good, and healing all that were oppressed of the devil; for God was with him (Acts 10:38).

And God wrought special miracles by the hands of Paul: So that from his body were brought unto the sick handkerchiefs or aprons, and the diseases departed from them, and the evil spirits went out of them (Acts 19:11,12).

So then faith cometh by hearing, and hearing by the word of God (Romans 10:17).

For the kingdom of God is not in word, but in power (1 Corinthians 4:20).

But we have this treasure in earthen vessels, that the excellency of the power may be of God, and not of us (2 Corinthians 4:7).

Now unto him that is able to do exceeding abundantly above all that we ask or think, according to the power that worketh in us (Ephesians 3:20).

But unto the Son he saith, Thy throne, O God, is for ever and ever: a sceptre of righteousness is the sceptre of thy kingdom. Thou hast loved righteousness, and hated iniquity; therefore God, even thy God, hath anointed thee with the oil of gladness above thy fellows (Hebrews 1:8,9).

Is any sick among you? let him call for the elders of the church; and let them pray over him, anointing him with oil in the name of the Lord: And the prayer of faith shall save the sick, and the Lord shall raise him up; and if he have committed sins, they shall be forgiven him (James 5:14, 15).

But ye have an unction from the Holy One, and ye know all things (1 John 2:20).

But the anointing which ye have received of him abideth in you, and ye need not that any man teach you: but as the same anointing teacheth you of all things, and is truth, and is no lie, and even as it hath taught you, ye shall abide in him (1 John 2:27).

Beloved, now are we the sons of God, and it doth not yet appear what we shall be: but we know that, when he shall appear, we shall be like him; for we shall see him as he is (1 John 3:2).

He that committeth sin is of the devil; for the devil sinneth from the beginning. For this purpose the Son of God was manifested, that he might destroy the works of the devil (1 John 3:8).

And they overcame him by the blood of the Lamb, and by the word of their testimony; and they loved not their lives unto the death (Revelation 12:11).

ENDNOTES

1. Kenneth W. Osbeck, *101 Hymn Stories*
   (Grand Rapids: Kregel Publications, 1982), 127.

2. Strong's Electronic Concordance (KJV).
   Copyright © 1989. 681

3. Bill Harmon © 1958.

4. Bible Illustrator for Windows Version 3.0f.
   Copyright © 1990–1998 by Parsons Technology Inc.

5. Written by Edward Mote (1797–1874).

6. See: www.geocities.com/bettybaxterstory/index2.html.

7. Kenneth W. Osbeck, *101 Hymn Stories*
   (Grand Rapids: Kregel Publications, 1982). 264, 267.

ABOUT THE AUTHOR

Rod Parsley is pastor of World Harvest Church in Columbus, Ohio, a dynamic megachurch with more than 12,000 in attendance weekly, that touches lives worldwide. He is also a highly sought-after crusade and conference speaker who delivers a life-changing message to raise the standards of physical purity, moral integrity and spiritual intensity.

Parsley also hosts Breakthrough, a daily and weekly television broadcast, seen by millions across America and around the world, as well as oversees Bridge of Hope Missions and Outreach, World Harvest Bible College and World Harvest Christian Academy. He and his wife, Joni, have two children, Ashton and Austin.

OTHER BOOKS BY ROD PARSLEY

40 Days to Your Promised Harvest

Backside of Calvary

Breakthrough Quotes

The Commanded Blessing

Covenant Blessings

Daily Breakthrough

The Day Before Eternity

God's Answer to Insufficient Funds

He Sent His Word and Healed Them

The Jubilee Anointing

My Promise Is the Palace, So What Am I
Doing in the Pit?

No Dry Season (best-seller)

No More Crumbs (best-seller)

On the Brink (#1 best-seller)

Power Through the Baptism
of the Holy Ghost

Renamed and Redeemed

Repairers of the Breach

Serious Survival Strategies

Ten Golden Keys to Your Abundance

Unclaimed Riches

Your Harvest is Come

For more information about Breakthrough, World
Harvest Church or to receive a product list of the many
books, audio and video tapes by Rod Parsley,
write or call:

Breakthrough
P.O. Box 32932
Columbus, Ohio 43232-0932
(614) 837-1990 (Office)

For information about World Harvest
Bible College, write or call:

World Harvest Bible College
P.O. Box 32901
Columbus, Ohio 43232-0901
(614) 837-4088

If you need prayer, Breakthrough Prayer Warriors
are ready to pray with you
24 hours a day, 7 days a week at:
(614) 837-3232

Visit Rod Parsley at his website address:
www.breakthrough.net

RECENT MINISTRY TOOLS BY ROD PARSLEY

Your Harvest is Come

God is looking to give birth to a revolutionary remnant who will thrust in the sickle and reap their three-fold harvest. In this book you will learn how to: Give birth to a three-fold harvest: spiritually, physically and financially; receive an impartation of faith passed down from generation to generation to reap the end time harvest; and speak the Word of God in faith over your seed.

BK 929 (book)..**$5**

God's Got You Covered ... Learning How to Abide Under the Shadow of the Almighty

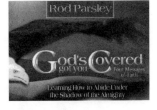

You are protected by God above, protected by God below, protected by God in front and protected by God behind. Get the revelation on this 4-tape audio series down into your spirit and move into the new dimension that God has destined for you!

TS 140 (audio)..**$20**

Hand in Hand

Whether you're married, single, young or old, you'll discover how you can live a victorious Christian life through the solid, biblical wisdom Pastor Rod and Joni Parsley have gleaned from their years of family ministry together in this 4-tape series.

TS 134 (audio)................................**$20**
VS 59 (video)................................**$60**

Hidden for You

Pastor Parsley plumbs the depths of God's Word in this 2-tape audio series to help you understand that the mysteries of God aren't hidden from you . . . they are hidden for you.

TS 137 (audio).......................................$10

On the Brink

In the early dawn of this new millennium, we sense a stirring within ourselves, an uneasiness that alerts us to the shifting winds of time. This book is a powerful look at how we as Christians must face the challenges of living in these last days.

BK 935 (book)...$20

Overthrowing the Spirit of Debt

It's time to get mad at the devil, overthrow the spirit of debt, and learn how to position yourself for overflowing financial blessing. Discover how to break the curse of lack. This book will teach you the simple act of faith and obedience to loose God's storehouse of financial blessing.

MB 8 (book)...$5

(PLEASE PRINT CLEARLY)

(Circle One)
Mr. Mrs. Ms.

Name _____ Phone:(_____) _____

Address _____ Apt. _____

City _____ State _____ Zip _____

GEN1RP

QTY	ITEM #	TITLE/DESCRIPTION	COST	TOTAL

SHIPPING & HANDLING	
Order Value	**Shipping Cost**
0 - $50.00	$10.00
$51.00-$100.00	$15.00
$100+	$20.00
International Orders - Call for freight charges	

SUBTOTAL	
SHIPPING & HANDLING:	
TOTAL	

MAIL TO: *BREAKTHROUGH* , P.O. Box 32932,
Columbus, OH 43232-0932, USA
Visit us on the web at **www.breakthrough.net**

Make checks payable to *BREAKTHROUGH* or pay by Credit Card.

❏ CHECK/MONEY ORDER ❏ VISA ❏ MasterCard ❏ DISCOVER ❏ 🔵

Card Number _____ _____ _____ _____

Name on Card_____Exp. Date:_____

Signature _____

Call **1-800-637-2288** for faster service on Credit Card orders only!